Searching for
Chipeta

Dedication

I dedicate this book to Chipeta, a woman, a wife, a mother, and the ultimate humanitarian; to C. J. Brafford and O. Roland McCook Sr.; and to the Ute men, women, and children whose original ancestors lived in the Land of the Shining Mountains, long before any others. Thank you for your patience, your valuable time and knowledge, and for your friendship. Here's to the good road ahead of us all.

V. L. K.

THE STORY OF A UTE AND HER PEOPLE

Searching for Chipeta

Vickie Leigh Krudwig

Fulcrum Publishing
Golden, Colorado

Library of Congress Cataloging-in-Publication Data
    Krudwig, Vickie Leigh, 1957-
        Searching for Chipeta : the story of a Ute and her people / Vickie Leigh Krudwig.
            p. cm.
        ISBN 1-55591-466-7
        1. Chipeta, 1843-1924—Juvenile literature.
2. Tabeguache women—Biography—Juvenile literature.
3. Tabeguache Indians—History—Juvenile literature.
4. Tabeguache Indians—Government relations—Juvenile literature. 5. Ouray—Juvenile literature.
[1. Chipeta, 1843-1924. 2. Tabeguache Indians. 3. Ute Indians. 4. Indians of North America. 5. Women—Biography.]   I.
    Title.
    E99.T114.C455 2004
    979.004'974576—dc22
    [B]
    2003023796

Printed in the United States of America
0 9 8 7 6 5 4 3 2

Editorial: Susan Hill Newton
Design: Ann W. Douden and Jack Lenzo
Cover and title page photographs: "Chepetta" by F.S. Balster. Copyright © Denver Public Library, Western History Collection, #Z-56

Fulcrum Publishing
16100 Table Mountain Parkway, Suite 300
Golden, Colorado 80403
(800) 992-2908 • (303) 277-1623
www.fulcrum-books.com

ACKNOWLEDGMENTS *To my husband, Mark, and my children, Jessica, Rebecca, and Benjamin, who have been my constant and faithful companions on this remarkable journey to learn about Chipeta. I thank them for their love and support while I traveled for research and while I wrote this manuscript.*

To my parents, George and Alice Douthit, who encouraged me at a young age to learn about Colorado's native people and their amazing lives. I am grateful for the numerous family trips that allowed me to get a glimpse of history as it unfolded over the years. Your companionship on trips and your encouragement to follow my dream helped make this book possible.

To Valorie, Garry, Sean, Sasha, Tessa Mae, Veronica, Gary, Jeff, Krystal, Greg, Candice, Arturo, Elisyo, Antonio, Alana Marie, George, Cheryl, Chas, Laura, Kathrine Mae, John, James, Connie, Vic, Kent, and Rhonda. I appreciate your willingness to be a part of this experience and for your unbelievable support! I love all of you and feel great pride that you are a part of my unique heritage!

To Frank Lloyd Kramer and Lynn Suave, thank you for your unfailing friendship and support. You are a constant source of inspiration!

To Merline, Ronnie, Marie L., LeeAnn, Carol, Kerry, Carole B., Judy, Colton, Russ, Terry, Amy, Brian, Doug, and Alex, and to my critique group for being there for me throughout this project. Thank you for your support, prayers, and for taking over some of my responsibilities while I traveled and worked on this project. I love you all very much.

To Bob Baron, Sam Scinta, Susan Hill Newton, Marlene Blessing, and Daniel Forrest-Bank for their faith in this book and for their willingness to acknowledge the often forgotten past of Chipeta and the Ute people.

To the Friends of the Ute, and to numerous museum curators and librarians who assisted me as I did my research. I send a special thanks to the Ute Museum in Montrose, the Western History division of the Denver Public Library, the Colorado Historical Society, the Utah Historical Society, and to all the individuals who took the time to record history through their writing and documentaries.

Contents

WHEN I THINK OF HISTORY, I SEE IT FROM a twenty-first century point of view. Today we have the capability to record history through a variety of ways—magazines, newspapers, books, television, and radio to name a few. Proud parents videotape their children as they sing, laugh, and celebrate important milestones in their lives. Reporters take us to the front lines of war, with their live coverage, as history is taking place. We are even privy to witness history-making events worldwide as they actually occur, from the comfort of our own homes.

Hundreds of years ago, when the Ute people and other native tribes roamed the lands of Colorado, there were none of these devices to record their histories. Instead, the Ute elders preserved their past by retelling and passing along their stories from one generation to another. Stone petroglyphs also reveal the past in the canyons of Colorado and Utah with evidence of the earliest historians' efforts as they scratched important moments into the surface of the red sandstone rocks.

Countless books have been written about Colorado and the people who resided here. Many of the authors that penned the historical accounts have written them out of their passion for history and with the hope of preserving the past. It is in this same spirit that I wrote *Searching for Chipeta*. Although this book is based entirely on the actual history of Chipeta, there are many descriptions and emotions throughout the book that have been fabricated for the reader's advantage.

As a Colorado native, I have had the opportunity of knowing the rugged and beautiful mountains and valleys intimately. I have spent countless hours hiking and camping in the high mountain meadows near Buena Vista and Salida. And I have hunted for arrowheads with my parents on the low-lying lands east of Colorado Springs. These are my homelands—the very same ones that once belonged to the Ute people.

On my many trips throughout Colorado and Utah, I have tried to put myself in Chipeta's place, as a woman, wife, and mother. It was not difficult to imagine the pain of losing a son or a husband. I believe I understand Chipeta's love for her family as she took care of them and prayed for Creator to take care of her loved ones. I have also tried to feel her ties to the land.

In Montrose, I was overcome with emotion at the breathtaking views of the Uncompahgre River Valley, and the gorgeous snowcapped San Juan Mountains. It was not difficult to understand Chipeta's deep love and respect for the land. In my mind I could see her grief-stricken face as she passed by the old homestead headed for the reservations following the loss of her husband. As I rode the westbound train to Utah, I could hardly believe the change in the landscape. Lush green valleys soon disappeared as I crossed the Colorado River and headed into Utah. There were few trees if any, and wildlife was almost nonexistent. There were miles of dry and desolate wastelands. I felt a sense of apprehension as I thought of Chipeta and the Ute men, women, and children as they crossed the border into unwelcoming lands.

Words can hardly express the sights, sounds, and emotions that I experienced as I followed Chipeta's life and that of the Ute people. *Searching for Chipeta* was not just a project for me, but also a soul-searching journey of understanding the Ute culture and trying to comprehend the devastation they faced as they were forced out of Colorado. The actual dates and experiences included in the book come from three years of research and travels, and by interviewing Chipeta's great-great-grandson, O. Roland McCook Sr., and C. J. Brafford, an Ogallala Lakota Sioux and curator of the Ute Indian Museum. I have tried to be compassionate and respectful, while weaving bits and pieces of Ute customs and traditions into the book.

Every effort was made to create an accurate and factual story. However, no two historians are alike. Research materials written by both non-natives and the Utes themselves helped me as I prepared the book, as well as Roland's generous time and efforts to verify the validity of my accounts. Stories about Chipeta and the Utes are as diverse as the authors who write them. It is from my point of view, and my love of Chipeta and the great state of Colorado, that I offer you this account of Chipeta's life.

Sheep graze near the old Los Piños Agency near Saguache. (Courtesy Vickie Leigh Krudwig collection)

Chapter 1

PEOPLE OF THE SHINING MOUNTAINS

CHIPETA'S HANDS TREMBLED WITH excitement as she tied her buckskin baby doll securely into its cradleboard. This was the day she and her family had waited for.

Icy cold water ran high and swift along the banks of the Arkansas River as the snows were melting in the high country. It was the time of the Summer Moon, when the leaves came out. Mother Earth was awakening after the long winter months. Tender green shoots of grass and wild asparagus poked their sleepy heads out of the soil, reaching for the sun.

Mah mah' que ats, Magpie, squawked loudly as he bounced from limb to limb in a nearby piñon tree. His black and white feathers shimmered in the morning light. He, too, could sense the eagerness in the people. Magpie cocked his head and called out to the group below. No one seemed to hear him. They were too busy preparing for the journey.

People of the Tabeguache village hustled back and forth. Leaders had decided it was time to break camp and begin the journey to their summer grounds, in the central Rocky Mountains. The Tabeguache band of Utes was one of twelve bands who lived in parts of Utah, Wyoming, New Mexico, and most of Colorado.

Chipeta's mother moved quickly to gather up all of her family's belongings. They were taken out of the teepee and packed into parfleches (pouches) and baskets. Once everything was packed and the food baskets secured, they were set aside. It was time to take the teepee down.

Mother, Aunt, and Grandmother pulled at the bulky elk hides that covered their lodge. When the wooden poles of their lodge were completely exposed, they were unlashed and taken down.

Chipeta grasped the end of a log with both hands. She helped Mother pull it toward a brown and white pony that stood nearby. Together they carefully tied a thin pole onto each side of the creature. When the timbers were secure, the women draped the teepee coverings over the frame, making a travois.

The women laughed and chatted among themselves while they arranged their possessions carefully onto the travois. As the women continued to work, Chipeta tended to her younger brother, John McCook. She did not want him to stray away from the camp or go toward the fast-flowing river, where water babies waited to steal children.

While she waited, Chipeta picked up her toy cradleboard and rocked it back and forth in her arms. Her doll, too, would go to the "Land of the Shining Mountains." Chipeta ran her long, slender finger over the colorful glass beads on the cradleboard. Mother had made it for her seven winters ago. Row upon row of dazzling glass beads were skillfully sewn onto the buckskin that covered its frame. She was lucky to have gotten such a beautiful gift from Mother.

Chipeta pulled the cradleboard and baby onto her back. This was how her mother had carried her nine winters ago, after her birth. She had been a summer baby, born on June 10, 1843, according to the white man's calendar. Her Tabeguache family lived along the Los Piños River, near Conejos.

Chipeta's brother of only three winters was growing restless, squirmed away from his sister, and moved toward Mother. Chipeta tugged at John and gently pulled the toddler onto her lap. He protested by crying out. Quickly and affectionately Chipeta tapped the little boy's lips to quiet him. She sang him a song about the journey ahead. Her song was sweet and comforting, and John quickly settled down. He leaned against Chipeta, while Mother added the last of their household belongings onto the travois.

Sapavanero, Chipeta's older brother who had turned twenty winters, was tending to their family's horses. He was making sure that the animals were in good condition for their passage into the high country. Sapavanero waited eagerly for the signal to progress.

Magpie called again. This time he flew from the old gnarled piñon tree to the ground a few feet from Chipeta and her brother. Magpie had gathered too many twigs in his large pointed beak, yet he added one stick after another. Magpie was greedy. When he opened his beak to pick up one more twig, all of the others fell out.

Both Chipeta and John laughed at the silly bird as he hopped back and forth, picking up his earthly treasures. When he was finished, Magpie flew up into his tree and skillfully wove his sticks into a large bundle of twigs and grass. Chipeta smiled; Magpie was building his summer home. He would soon find a mate.

Chipeta's heart overflowed with joy. Magpie was a good thing to see. Grandfather once told her that *Mah mah' que ats* was an excellent messenger. Even though Magpie stole food and small trinkets from the people, he was also useful. Magpie warned other animals and the people of hidden dangers as they traveled along their ancestral trails. The birds, Grandfather said, were wise, too. They were able to overcome problems when they occurred.

Magpie was similar to her own people, thought Chipeta. They too had learned to triumph over difficulties when they occurred. That was how her people survived for so long. During the long winter months when times were hard, the Utes were always resourceful.

When food was scarce, they had learned to harvest the seeds, berries, roots, and insects that Creator had made. When shelters were lacking, Utes used trees and their branches to make wickiups to keep them out of the elements. Like Magpie, the people were able to adapt.

Change was in the air. The chill of winter was gone, and the delightful warm weather put everyone in a festive mood. Women and children gathered together in small groups. They waited for the sign to move forward.

Men, young and old, had talked among themselves making plans for their seasonal passage. Some of the young men had hunted small game in order to sustain the family as they traveled. They wanted to be sure everyone stayed safe as they moved to the north.

At last, it was time to leave. Everyone moved into line and slowly moved forward. Chipeta picked up John and carried him to the travois. She hoisted him up among the blankets and baskets and tied him into place with a rawhide robe. This would keep her little brother safe while they traveled.

Mother nodded and approved of Chipeta's good deed. She was grateful for the help while she prepared for the trip. Children were sometimes trampled by the horses if they got underfoot. Chipeta's abilities to care for children pleased her. Someday she would make a fine mother.

Chipeta glanced back at the long procession of people and horses. The image reminded her of an immense snake crawling across the land. Some of the older women and small children rode on the travois, while others walked or rode their ponies alongside them. The long column of people moved slowly and carefully over the terrain.

The Tabeguache family had grown a great deal. There were nearly thirty people in their close-knit family. Aunts, uncles, cousins, Grandfather, and Grandmother, in addition to her own brothers and her parents, had wintered in the lowlands near the Los Piños River, where winters were milder.

The San Juan Mountains had provided the Utes with protection from the chilly north winds for hundreds of years. The rugged terrain acted as a barrier too, keeping the Utes isolated from many of the eastern foreigners who came to the region to trap beaver.

During the long winter months, when game was hard to find, the bands separated and scattered throughout the region. In winter, the land could not support the vast number of Utes who lived in the area. Too many people competed for the food sources. Instead, families created their own little communities during the wintry weather.

Chipeta thought of this as she rode a pony alongside the travois and along the old trail. Centuries of travel and poles from the travois had etched telltale grooves into the earth, marking her people's seasonal migrations. The trails led the people to a secluded valley along the Arkansas River. Its sacred waters flowed down from the snow-covered mountains that *Sinawaf*, Creator, had made.

As the trip progressed, the scenery changed a great deal. Instead of short dry clumps of buffalo grass and sagebrush, there were vast open fields of lush grasses and wildflowers. Blue lupine and red clumps of paintbrush grew abundantly across the landscape. Aspen trees packed in clusters on the hillsides, and their brilliant green leaves glittered in the sunlight. The valley had never been so beautiful.

Chipeta missed her friends and was anxious to see them again. She couldn't wait to show them her new moccasins. During the cold, dreary days, Mother helped her cut out her first moccasins from soft deerskin. She showed Chipeta how to shape and sew her moccasins. Chipeta had beaded them herself using some of the blue and green beads Mother had given her. She would show her friends and relatives how much she had grown.

Ecstatic people rushed into the field. Their long journey was over, and they had arrived safely. Ponies stopped to graze and drink from the river, their tails swishing at newly hatched flies. Butterflies and swallows hovered over the meadow. Magpie's brother flew overhead, landing on a large boulder. His tail dipped up and down as he cawed, announcing the arrival of the people.

Chipeta's moccasined feet pattered across the clearing. The beautiful colors were a welcome sight after the dismal brown and gray colors of winter. The child closed her eyes and inhaled. Chipeta wanted to make the moment last. She wished to remember the mixture of fragrances—damp earth, sweetgrass, sage, and pine.

Her heart beat like a drum. This was the land she loved. It had been their summer home for as long as she could remember. How wonderful it was to return. Chipeta lifted her face up toward Grandfather Sky. The sun's dazzling rays felt warm on her skin.

A gentle breeze blew out of the west. Strands of Chipeta's long black hair fell across her face. She swept the hair away with her hand and could not take her eyes off of the stunning scenery.

Wintry snows still frosted the tops of the granite mountain peaks. A waterfall roared up above. Its white, watery veil cascaded over the rocky cliffs and boulders and down the tree-lined slopes of the valley.

Chipeta gave thanks to Creator. Now she was free from the confines of a darkened winter teepee. The season had been particularly bitter, and there had been little time to play outdoors. Food had been scarce, and some of her family suffered from frostbite and illness. There had been many nights when she had gone to bed with an empty belly.

But the warm-weather months meant that there would be plenty of good things to eat. It also marked the time of year when family and friends gathered together after winter. Other bands of Utes would join them in the Arkansas Valley. Soon the hillsides and meadows would be bustling with activity. Chipeta could hardly wait.

ONCE THE PEOPLE REACHED THE
summer grounds, they quickly went about
the task of setting up camp. Chipeta helped
Mother and Grandmother unload the pony

drag. When she was finished, Chipeta kept an eye on John and her cousins
while the older women set up their lodges.

After the long pine poles were lifted off of the horses, the women tied
the ends of the poles together with braided rawhide ropes. Together they
lifted the frame into place, forming a tripod. The skeleton of their lodge was
set firmly into the ground, and Chipeta's mother and grandmother added the
other poles to form the rest of the structure. Painted hides were stretched over
the wooden structure and fastened with wooden pegs.

Once the teepee was complete, Chipeta, along with her cousins, helped
pick up stones and clean up the floor inside the dwelling. The children giggled as they trampled the soft meadow floor with their tiny feet, making it
firm and smooth.

Next they gathered willow branches from bushes along a nearby brook.
She and her mother tied them together with sinew and piled them along the
inside walls of the lodge. After the willow platforms were finished, the women
covered them with thick furry buffalo hides.

Chipeta took her doll out of her buckskin cradleboard. She patted her
baby's head and laid her down. She pretended to clean her baby and feed her.
After all, the long journey had made everyone hungry.

Setting up camp kept everyone busy, and the day had gone by quickly.
Other bands of Utes began to file into the area. Soon campfires were blazing
and hundreds of teepees stood silhouetted against the darkening night sky. The
empty meadow was now full with life, as the *Noochew*, the Utes, settled in for
the season.

Quaking aspen trees and towering ponderosa pine trees stood guard over
the people as they ate their evening meal. The Utes were content. There were

plenty of deer and mountain sheep to eat. The people relished the fresh asparagus and wild onions that Mother Earth had provided for them.

With full bellies, the people wrapped themselves in colorful wool shawls and blankets. Families clustered around large campfires to visit and catch up on the latest news. Chipeta sat next to her brothers and waited eagerly for Grandfather to tell a story.

In the distance a lonely coyote yipped and howled. Chipeta looked up at the dark towering mountain peak and then at the old man sitting in front of the fire. She wished Grandfather would again tell them the story of why *Yo go vits*, Coyote, howls. Chipeta shivered and wrapped her arms around her legs and waited. She watched as sparks from the fire drifted up into the dark night sky and disappeared among the stars.

Grandfather sat on an old brown buffalo robe in front of the fire. The flickering light of the campfire reflected in his dark brown eyes and across his face. He looked at Chipeta and nodded. The old one closed his eyes for a moment as he remembered the words of his ancestors. His voice was slow and steady. Everyone watched as he held up an old leather pouch.

"A long time ago, there were no people in the world," he began, "and *Sinawaf* was lonely, and he decided to make people." The elder picked up a twig and broke it in two. "Creator gathered up sticks and cut them into

Like this girl, Chipeta helped watch over her little brother while her mother performed other duties. (Courtesy of the Denver Public Library, Western History Collection, #X-30402)

many pieces. When he was done, he put the sticks into a bag, while his brother Coyote watched."

Chipeta watched as Grandfather put the sticks into the old brown pouch. He laid it on the ground in front of him. He paused for a minute and pulled his blanket up over his bony shoulders. Chipeta waited eagerly for the story-teller to continue.

"When the bag was filled with sticks, Creator closed it. He told Coyote not to open the bag. Then Creator went away leaving the bag of sticks behind."

"Well," said the old man, raising a finger over each ear, "nosey old Coyote picked up the bag and opened it."

Chipeta gasped and put her hands over her mouth. Her dark, almond-shaped eyes widened in surprise. Grandfather glanced over at the little girl and smiled.

"Coyote was astonished!" cried the old man. "Tiny people were inside the bag!"

"Ayee," cried Chipeta. She leaned forward. This was her favorite part of the story. People around the campfire laughed.

"The stick people quickly jumped out of the bag and began to speak in different languages," continued Grandfather. "Soon they began to fight each other. Coyote begged them to stop, but they did not listen! Again, Coyote pleaded for them to return. It was too late. The stick people had run away to different parts of the world."

"When Creator returned, he knew the bag had been opened. Coyote had not obeyed him. 'The nations were not prepared to come into the world,' said Creator. 'They were to be placed equally over the earth. The trouble you have caused will make wars. People will try to gain land from one another.' Creator punished Coyote and sent him away."

Grandfather looked at Chipeta. His eyes sparkled as he spoke. "This is why poor old Coyote howls at the sky. He wants to go home."

Chipeta nodded in agreement. She moved closer to her mother, while the old man continued. He picked up the worn pouch.

"Once Coyote was gone, Creator picked up the bag. He looked into it.

Deep inside remained a few of the stick people. They had not run away like the others."

Grandfather took a few sticks out of the bag and held them up for everyone to see. His voice was loud and strong. "'This small tribe will be known as the *Noochew*,' said Creator. Then he spoke to the tiny ones, 'You will be very bold, since the others are not complete, and you, the *Noochew*, will rise above them. I will place you high in the mountains so you will always be close to me.' That is how we came to live here, in the Land of the Shining Mountains," said the old man.

He made a sweeping gesture with his arms. "We have been here for as long as anyone can remember," he added. Everyone nodded in agreement.

Chipeta loved the story, as well as the sacred mountains of their ancestors. Her people had always lived here, and she too would grow old and die in the mountains. For that is how Creator had wanted it.

Chipeta stood up and walked toward the old man. She thanked Grandfather for his story and handed him a small bundle of braided sweetgrass. The elder was pleased and nodded, accepting the humble offering from the youngster. He reached out with his thin brown fingers and gently patted her head. Chipeta smiled and turned to join her mother and father. It was time to return to the lodge and rest.

In the quiet of the night, under a blanket of twinkling stars, the people slumbered. A gentle breeze rustled through pine boughs, and the sounds of babbling brooks and crickets lulled Chipeta and her people to sleep, while *Sinawaf* kept watch over his people.

CHIPETA, NOW FIFTEEN WINTERS, carefully made her way toward the marsh that lay alongside the Arkansas River. Her bare feet sunk down into the spongy brown soil as she stepped over the tangled mass of waterlogged grasses and roots. She carried a large brown basket made of willow and the curved digging stick her mother had made her.

Red-winged blackbirds cautiously clicked and whistled as Chipeta approached the water's edge. The birds wrapped their tiny claws around the reeds as they rode up and down on them in the breeze. Croaking bullfrogs and all kinds of birds filled the air with song. The wetlands became a symphony of serene sounds.

Gray clouds gathered over the mountains in the west, and the air smelled like rain. The young woman hastily began to gather her harvest. She planned to fill her baskets with cattail bulbs and shoots, and whatever else Creator would provide her.

Chipeta studied the digging stick in her hand. Its wood was worn and smooth from years of use. She was nine winters when her mother presented it to her. Together mother and daughter spent a wonderful day gathering wild onions and carrots.

At first the digging stick felt awkward in Chipeta's tiny hands. But as the day wore on she had become skillful at finding the tasty roots and bulbs. Over the years, Mother and Grandmother had shown her the location of hundreds of plants as they traveled. Each plant had its own purpose and its own season for harvest. They provided her people with food and medicines.

Chipeta held these details deep within her memory. If she were to forget the wisdom of her mother and grandmother, she would not be able to find these foods. Roots, bulbs, grass seeds, and flowers had sustained Chipeta's ancestors for centuries.

Her first harvest was a special time for her, as it brought her closer to becoming a young woman. Mother walked proudly next to her as the two returned to the camp. Chipeta's basket was so full she could hardly carry it.

At home, she ceremoniously sorted the fresh roots and onions into small parcels. She held her head high as she walked from teepee to teepee delivering her edible gifts. Chipeta's friends and family accepted the freshly harvested bulbs and shoots and thanked her. They were eager to celebrate the important milestone in the young girl's life. Creator would bless her with abundance because of her generosity.

Now, the fifteen-year-old prayed to Creator. She asked that he would help her find a great quantity of plants. She wanted to share them with her friend Black Mare, who was gravely ill. She had not been well since the birth of her son, Paron. There was a rumor that Black Mare had been bitten by a rattlesnake. Whatever was true, Chipeta knew that Black Mare's health was declining rapidly.

Chipeta set her basket down by the side of the shoreline. She pushed her digging stick into the murky, cold water. With a tap and a tug, Chipeta expertly lifted the cattail, root and all, out of the water. She set the plant next to the basket and continued to toil. The cattails were just right for harvest. Their tender green shoots would make an excellent salad, she thought. She would bake some of the bulbs and take them over to Black Mare and her husband, Ouray.

Chipeta knew Black Mare's condition only worsened with each day. Even the medicine man in the village could not make Black Mare well. Ouray's young wife was dying. Soon she would go to the Spirit World where their ancestors lived. Chipeta trembled and wiped a tear from her eye with the back of her hand. She didn't want to accept the reality of Black Mare's condition.

A light mist began to fall, and Chipeta knew that she must get back to camp. The morning was gray and cloudy and would probably be that way all day. Chipeta did not complain. She was grateful for the moisture. The land had been drier than normal, as drought had gripped parts of the region. Water was essential to her people, and she rejoiced when the tiny drops of water speckled her skin.

Chipeta put another clump of reeds onto the shoreline. Her basket was almost full. One more, she thought, as she reached for another clump. Just as her hand touched the cool green reeds, a cinnamon-colored ruddy duck burst through them. It frantically flapped its wings and quacked loudly at the intruder.

Caught off guard, Chipeta stumbled backwards into the water, dropping her digging stick. Her heart beat wildly and she paused to catch her breath. She laughed nervously and righted herself. Chipeta fumbled around for her digging stick. It lay wedged against a clump of reeds. She picked it up and parted the tall stalks with it.

To her surprise, the duck, a female, had laid a cluster of brown speckled eggs within the small clump of cattails. Delighted at the discovery, Chipeta carefully picked up one and examined it.

Rain came down in bigger drops and thunder rumbled in the distance. Chipeta put the egg back into the nest, careful not to disturb the others. Soon the eggs would hatch, and Mother Duck would be busy raising her little babies. Someday she would have children of her own to raise. Chipeta smiled at the thought as she quickly stepped her way across the marshy landscape and back onto shore. She gathered up the plants she had harvested and carefully arranged them in her basket. She picked up her bounty and moved in the direction of the village.

Chipeta's feet were cold and almost numb from wading in the icy water. Her buckskin dress was soaked, but she didn't care. Today she had plenty of food, and the roasted roots would taste wonderful on such a rainy day. Chipeta sidestepped puddles along the path. Mother Earth was thirsty. She wished that the rains could bring Black Mare back to health.

Chipeta remembered when her friend became ill. She had noticed that Black Mare's household duties were being neglected. Black Mare had tried to take care of things herself but couldn't; yet she was too proud to ask for help. Chipeta and Black Mare talked into the afternoon, while Paron sat next to his mother. Chipeta insisted that she help prepare dinner for her and Ouray. She told Black Mare to rest while she cooked and cleaned and kept an eye on Paron.

The sickness had taken its toll, and Black Mare grew weaker with each passing day. Now Ouray's wife was unable to get out of bed. It pained Chipeta to see her friend like this. She recalled her visit with Black Mare a few days before. Embarrassed at her condition, the poor woman had apologized for not making tea for Chipeta's visit. Black Mare had cried in shame.

Although she was older, Black Mare had grown up with Chipeta. They were like sisters. The girls worked side by side under sunny blue skies as they tanned hides.

Black Mare and Chipeta often gathered plants together, laughing and talking about their futures. The girls talked about marriage and children. They both agreed that they would be good Ute wives to their husbands. Now Chipeta gathered plants by herself.

Chipeta had learned much over the years. Her life as a Tabeguache Ute had been a good one. So many people in her tribe had played an important role in her life. As a young girl, she had learned many important lessons by watching the older men and women in camp.

A smile flashed across Chipeta's face. The doll and cradleboard that Mother had given her had prepared her for motherhood. As she played with her buckskin doll, she was learning how to be a good mother. She would use these skills to help Black Mare and Ouray. She would help take care of Black Mare's boy.

Over the weeks, Chipeta visited Black Mare often. At first Paron was shy and hid behind his mother whenever Chipeta came into the lodge. He cried when Chipeta tried to bathe him or feed

Cradleboards kept babies close to their mothers, safe and secure. (Courtesy of the Colorado Historical Society, #F-7699)

him. Over time, though, Paron grew accustomed to Chipeta's daily visits. He watched as Chipeta mended and sewed clothes for the family and tended to Black Mare's needs.

The young girl made wild peppermint tea and gave it to Black Mare to soothe her stomach. Chipeta's constant companionship comforted Black Mare, and she was filled with gratitude. Ouray, just twenty-five winters, was grateful too. He appreciated having someone to watch over his ill wife and son. It allowed him to go out hunting and deal with important tribal issues, as Ouray's status in the tribe was rising.

The rain came down in larger drops now, and Chipeta walked faster toward her camp. In the distance Chipeta could see the smoke from their early morning campfires drifting sluggishly into the gray skies. She paused to catch her breath and shift the contents of her basket. Her body shivered from the damp, and she was anxious to get back to the village. She would take food to Black Mare as soon as she could.

When she approached camp, Chipeta's heart thudded against her chest. Her eyes widened in disbelief. People in her village had moved their teepees far away from Black Mare's lodge. Chipeta dropped her basket and wailed loudly. Death had taken her friend away from her. She ran across the soggy ground toward Black Mare's teepee. A medicine man stepped out into the rain, shaking his head. Chipeta pushed past the man and into the teepee.

Chipeta's brown eyes filled with tears. Her childhood friend, her sister, was gone forever. She knelt next to Ouray and quietly placed her hand on his shoulder. Ouray wept, while Paron bawled. The wails of his grandmother and aunts had frightened the boy. He cried for his mother and could not be comforted. Chipeta picked the little boy up and held him close. She carried Paron back to her lodge, while Black Mare's family prepared her body for burial.

The rain continued late into the afternoon. Chipeta took her knife out of its sheath. She held it up to her long black hair and began slashing at it. Soon the silky locks of hair lay in a pile on the floor of the teepee.

Chipeta would help Ouray and Black Mare's grieving family prepare her body for burial. She walked slowly toward their lodge. She felt apprehensive, as she knew the ghosts of ancestors lingered there, waiting to show Black Mare the way to the Spirit World.

Black Mare's body was placed on a blanket. Her friends and family lovingly surrounded her, setting some of her personal belongings next to her. Chipeta watched as Black Mare's bone awl and needles were tenderly laid next to her friend. She would need these things as she traveled through the underworld.

Chipeta shook uncontrollably and wailed as the blanket was wrapped tightly around her friend's body. Rawhide ropes were stretched around the corpse to keep the body and contents of the blankets from being exposed. The scene in the teepee seemed unreal to Chipeta as Black Mare's body was lifted from her bed.

People watched in silence as Ouray, Paron, Chipeta, and the rest of Black Mare's family slowly carried her body away from the encampment. They sang mournful songs as they walked alongside the body. Chills ran down Chipeta's spine as she thought of the underworld. Black Mare's body was quietly placed in a crevice a few miles from their camp. No one spoke on the way back.

Black Mare's possessions were removed from her lodge and set on fire. Chipeta watched as the raging flames devoured them. The thick black smoke burned her eyes and lungs. Chipeta worried about Ouray and his young son. Who would care for them? She had grown fond of the baby boy.

Chipeta remembered Paron's birth with fondness. It was a celebrated event in the village. Black Mare had given Ouray a healthy boy, and he was the couple's pride and joy. Black Mare would not see her young boy grow into manhood, and she would not grow old with Ouray. Pain and sadness washed over Chipeta, matching the gray and somber skies.

Grief stricken and alone, Ouray returned to their empty lodge. He seemed lost without his wife. He and his young son needed Chipeta more than ever. The young Ute maiden would never leave Paron and Ouray in their time of sorrow. She would honor her friend Black Mare by taking care of their needs.

Chapter 4

IT WAS DUSK, AND THE SUN WAS beginning to dip behind the lavender-colored hills in the west. Chipeta watched as the sky turned a gorgeous red and gold color. She paused to take in the moment. The sun's golden rays reached far across the evening sky, illuminating millions of cottonwood seeds as they floated effortlessly in the air. The tiny seeds reminded her of fluffy white snowflakes that fell in the wintertime.

Chipeta set Paron down on a soft hide near the river's edge. She set the soap root and soft skins down next to her and proceeded to undress the little boy. Once he was naked, Chipeta began the process of bathing Paron. She pounded the soap root into a soft, foamy lather.

Paron's eyes grew wide in amazement as Chipeta spread the soft suds over his tiny arms and legs. He held on to Chipeta's sleeve, and his teeth chattered as Chipeta rinsed the suds from his body. When Chipeta tried to apply the suds to Paron's round face, he scowled and pushed her hand away. The little one moved his head from side to side, trying to avoid the soapy doeskin. Chipeta laughed at the boy's stubbornness. She studied his lean, brown body, and she was pleased that the little boy was healthy and growing.

When Paron was scrubbed clean, Chipeta gathered him into her arms and wrapped a soft piece of doeskin around his body. She lifted him onto her right hip and headed back toward the encampment. In the distance, Chipeta could see the wood smoke from her cooking fire drifting out of the teepee's flap. Her heart skipped a beat at the sight. She still found it odd to be taking care of Black Mare's boy and Ouray's household.

It had been months since Black Mare's death, and Chipeta and Ouray did not speak of her. To talk of the dead was dangerous and often resulted in death for the mourner who refused to let go. Chipeta felt herself shiver. She tried to forget the death of Black Mare but could not. She wondered if her friend's soul had made its way safely through the underground passages to the world of spirits.

Somewhere in the trees above her, a night bird called out. Its shrill screech startled her. Chipeta picked up speed. The thought of wandering spirits frightened her, making the hair on her arms stand up. She cautiously made her way up the darkening path, glancing from side to side and holding Paron close to her.

Relief washed over Chipeta when she and Paron reached the teepee. Once inside, she set the boy down and he ran toward Ouray. Chipeta laughed at Paron as he climbed upon Ouray's strong shoulders, pulling at his long black hair. Father and son playfully wrestled with each other. It warmed Chipeta's heart to see the close bond that Ouray shared with his young son.

Ouray grabbed Paron and set him down on the sleeping robes. His dark eyes followed Chipeta's movements as she put away the soap root and damp skins. She picked up a rabbit skin blanket to wrap Paron in. The little boy quickly scrambled out of her reach. He squealed in delight as he hid himself under a buffalo blanket.

Chipeta smiled and winked at Ouray. She called for the little boy in a worried voice. Paron giggled but did not move or answer her. Chipeta lifted the lids on her baskets, pretending to look for Ouray's son.

Finally Chipeta moved toward Paron's hiding pace. Ouray's eyes danced with laughter as Chipeta pulled the robe off. He chuckled as Chipeta snatched the youngster up into her arms and held him close. The laughter was welcome after the long, gloomy months following his wife's death.

When Paron finally surrendered to Chipeta, she wrapped him snugly into the soft, furry blanket. The young woman spoke quietly to Paron as she slowly traced her finger across his tiny forehead and around his almond-shaped eyes. The boy's eyelids drooped as Chipeta rocked him back and forth.

Orange and yellow flames from the cooking fire crackled and popped as they devoured the cedar and pine branches in the pit. The firelight flickered, making shadows dance across their faces. Paron's eyes grew heavy with sleep. Chipeta leaned over Paron and stroked his soft black hair, and soon he was fast asleep in Chipeta's lap.

Chipeta laid him in his sleeping place and covered him with a warm blanket. She studied Paron's peaceful face. Chipeta glanced up at Ouray. His eyes were focused on her, and his face was full of tenderness.

Ouray stooped over his son and gently touched his cheek. Chipeta blushed as Ouray thanked her for taking good care of his son. He was grateful for her kindness. He moved toward the back of the teepee to smoke his pipe. The familiar smell of the tobacco was reassuring to Chipeta. She could picture her father sitting in front of their evening fire, smoking his pipe.

As smoke from Ouray's pipe rose upward, Chipeta offered silent prayers for her ancestors and for Black Mare. She prayed for Ouray, and for Paron. She hoped that Creator would bless them all with a good way of life.

As a young girl, she had always cherished the quiet evenings at home when the family gathered safely together after a long and busy day. Chipeta smiled as she recalled the hushed voices of her parents as they talked about their day while she and her brothers lay in their beds.

Chipeta stretched for a moment and yawned. She picked up a basket filled with pieces of buckskin. She sat down close to Ouray. He watched her as she opened a smaller pouch and took out a bone awl. Chipeta was making new moccasins for Paron. The little one had already outgrown his clothing.

Ouray smiled at her. In the stillness of the nighttime, while Paron slept, Chipeta and Ouray talked about the day's events. They talked fondly of Paron and his awkward attempt to catch a grasshopper earlier that day.

These were the times Chipeta cherished most. She enjoyed Ouray's company. Not only was the young man handsome, he was intelligent too. And Ouray treated her with an unusual amount of respect. He seemed interested in everything she said or did. Chipeta felt a tremendous satisfaction at the thought.

As she punched the sharp point of the awl into the leather, Chipeta remembered her first few conversations with Ouray, shortly after Black Mare's death. At first the words were few. They were awkward ones, and she and Ouray spoke mostly of Paron, the weather, and said very little about themselves.

But in time Ouray brought details of council meetings into their conversation. Her mind reeled as Ouray talked of the eastern foreigners who invaded the Utes' lands. She had struggled to grasp Ouray's reasoning. Why would he share such important details with her, a woman? Crucial issues such as these were left to the men of the tribe. Women she knew had no say in such matters. Yet Ouray continued to inform Chipeta about the changes taking place. In the privacy of their teepee, they spent long hours discussing and debating the issues facing their people.

It was through their long talks that Chipeta uncovered the mysterious facts of Ouray's life. Ouray's father, Guerra Murah (also called Salvadore), was an Apache. He had been taken by the Tabeguache Utes when he was a little boy. Guerra was adopted into the tribe and raised according to Tabeguache traditions. He later married a Tabeguache maiden. Guerra and his wife lived near Taos, New Mexico, with his wife's family.

Before long, Guerra had gained the respect of the people in his community. Over the years he eventually rose in rank, becoming a sub-chief of the Tabeguache people.

Ouray came into the world on a cold, clear night on November 13, 1833, while the mysterious Leonid meteor showers streaked across the dark sky. Chipeta pondered the timing of Ouray's birth. She remembered how the elders talked of the strange lights that flashed across the night skies.

Six years after he was born, his mother had given birth to

Ouray returned to the Ute people when he was seventeen (1850). (Courtesy of the Denver Public Library, Western History Collection, #X-30584) another boy named Quenche. Shortly after his birth, Ouray's mother died, leaving Guerra, Ouray, and Quenche to fend for themselves.

Sadness of the memory was still written across Ouray's handsome face when he recounted the details of how the women of the Tabeguache community had quickly tended to his broken family, just as Chipeta now cared for Ouray and Paron.

A lump grew in Chipeta's throat as she recalled these stories. History had repeated itself. To Chipeta, these stories were also reminders that Ouray had once loved another woman. Filled with compassion, Chipeta reached toward Ouray, patting his arm. The young brave looked into her face, unaware of the thoughts that were passing through her mind. Ouray placed his own calloused hand upon Chipeta's. Her mind wandered back to his story.

Ouray's father had remarried, and a few years later, in 1845, Ouray's half-sister, Susan, was born. After a couple of years, Ouray's parents returned to their Tabeguache family in the San Juan region.

Chipeta had been horrified when Ouray explained that he and his brother had been left in the hands of some Spanish ranchers while their parents moved on. In exchange for a "white education," the two brothers would work as sheepherders and do other domestic chores.

It was during that time that Ouray and Quenche both learned to speak the Spanish language. Jesuit priests taught the boys how to speak a little bit of English as well.

By seventeen, Ouray had grown restless. The life he lived in Taos could not compare with the life his father led in the San Juan Mountains. Guerra's carefree way of life appealed to Ouray. The thought of hunting, riding horses, and fighting had captured his imagination.

One day, Ouray abandoned his Spanish home in Taos and headed north. For days the young man rode alone over the rugged desert landscape. He was anxious to join his father, mother, and sister in the San Juan territory.

Quenche could not be persuaded to join Ouray. He had grown accustomed to the Mexican people there, and he preferred their way of living to that of his Ute people. Sadly, Ouray's brother stayed in Taos while Ouray moved on. Quenche settled into the area and became a peddler. He loaded his burros with piñon wood and sold it to the citizens of Taos.

Chipeta grinned as she recounted the fact that she was just seven winters when Ouray rode into their camp. His arrival, she told him, had caused quite a commotion. Everyone in the village had talked about it, including Black Mare and many of the young maidens.

His father, too, had been overjoyed to see him, as were his stepmother and sister. It thrilled them to know that Ouray had grown into a fine young man. His return to the Tabeguache community was a turning point for the young man, and Ouray had adapted easily to the lifestyles and customs of his Ute family.

Shortly after Ouray's return, Guerra died, leaving each of his boys several prized ponies. Suddenly Ouray was a wealthy young man. His skills as a hunter and a rider were admired by many people in the encampment. People talked favorably of Ouray's gallantry. Many of the young women in the village dreamed of becoming Ouray's wife.

Chipeta and Ouray watched the fire in the pit as it grew dimmer. The evening had passed quickly. It was late and time to retire. Tomorrow would be another busy day for both of them. Ouray had plans to hunt bighorn sheep in the high country with his uncle and cousin; Chipeta had to take care of Paron and harvest grass seeds before they were blown away.

After she carefully put her sewing away, Chipeta climbed under her sleeping skins. Her eyes strained to adjust to the darkness of the teepee. She held her hand up in front of her face. The teepee was so dark that Chipeta could not see it.

A cool gust of wind rushed in through the smoke flap, and Chipeta pulled her robe up over her shoulders. She lay awake listening to the sounds of the wind as it rattled the elk skin lodge. Leaves and bushes rustled, and the cricket's song was slow and deliberate. Summer was almost over and once again change was in the air.

Sleep would not come easily to Chipeta. Her mind raced back to the past when Ouray had come back to her people. She pictured the look on Ouray's face as he had listened to the elders tell stories of the old times. Like her,

Ouray treasured the Utes' legends and histories. He had asked the elders many questions about the Tabeguache ancestors. Ouray wanted to learn everything he could about his people.

Not only had Ouray won the respect of Chief Nevava and most of the Ute community, he had gained the respect of Chipeta too. She was awed by his commitment to the Tabeguache people. His interest in the affairs of the Utes was unwavering.

Chipeta was thankful that she had been given the chance to help Ouray and Paron through their difficult time. Throughout their ordeal, her life had become full of meaning, and she would stay with Ouray and Paron for as long as they needed her. Chipeta hoped that it would be forever.

Chapter 5

BEAR DANCE

IT WAS STILL DARK WHEN Chipeta rose from her sleeping place. She dressed quickly and quietly, then felt her way across the unlit lodge, pausing when her hand touched its target. Chipeta picked up the pine-pitch water basket and moved slowly to the doorway. As she lifted the leather flap, the fresh morning air filled the teepee.

The sun was beginning to rise in the east, shrouding the earth and sky in a golden hue. The view was breathtaking. Swirls of gray mist wafted up from the ground and off of the red sandstone walls of the canyon as the sun's luminous rays warmed Mother Earth.

Chipeta strolled down the rock-strewn trail toward the river. There was no reason to rush, as Ouray and Paron were already up and tending to the horses. The sun would not catch them in bed, she thought to herself as she made her way down the trail. To do so meant lost opportunities, for the animals they depended upon for food and clothing hid during the daylight hours.

The damp red earth stained the bottoms of Chipeta's moccasins as she traveled over the path. Sunlight filtered through the old gnarled junipers and aspen that grew alongside the trail, and she welcomed its heat on her chilled face and arms.

Chipeta stopped for a moment to remove a tiny pebble from her moccasin. She sat down on a large gray boulder covered with light-green lichen. She slowly unlaced the leather ties of her moccasin and slid it off of her foot. Chipeta took a moment to catch her breath and to look at the scenery.

The solitude was welcome, as the last several months had been chaotic. Not only had she taken over Ouray's household, she was now his wife, and mother to Paron. Chipeta's responsibilities had grown considerably. Ouray traveled a great deal, leaving her to tend to Paron and to the household. Ouray kept busy trying to soothe tensions between the newcomers and his own people.

Chipeta held the annoying stone in her hand and studied it for a moment. The tiny stone reminded her of the miners and traders who traveled into their territories. At first they came in small numbers, and their existence did not worry many of the Utes. Her people outnumbered the outsiders considerably. Now the continuous western flow of outsiders had become intrusive like the pebble in her moccasin.

The gold rush in the central and southern mountains had created a frenzy of unwanted activity. Miners and settlers continued to take over the Utes' hunting grounds. The deer and elk and other game they had depended upon for ages were being hunted by the large numbers of newcomers. The vast herds of animals had diminished dramatically. The Tabeguache band of Utes had grown considerably over the years, with their numbers reaching more than 2,000 people, meaning many mouths to feed.

Chipeta remembered her early experiences with hunger. There were times during the cold winter months when she and her brothers had gone to bed with empty bellies. Her mother ate little so that her children could eat something. Everyone struggled to find food.

The stone suddenly seemed hard and cold in Chipeta's hands. She tossed the rock into the grass, where it quickly disappeared. Chipeta brushed her foot off and put her moccasin back on. She leaned forward to tie the leather laces and wished that the white people had never discovered their homelands. Haunting rumors continued to spread throughout the camps. Fifty thousand easterners had moved into the Utes' lands on the east side of the Rockies. Chipeta did not know if the stories were true or not, but the thought of so many foreigners unnerved her.

Getting back on the trail, Chipeta slowed her breathing and her pace. She needed the time to calm herself. She gladly embraced the beautiful morning. Chipeta decided she would leave her worries behind her, like the pebble from her moccasin. She walked down the trail with her empty water basket. She would not allow anything else to ruin her day.

Lavender pascal flowers and wild daisies dotted the grassy clearings that lay between the trees and boulders. Chipeta marveled at the glistening dewdrops hanging on the new blades of greening grass and yucca that grew along the pathway. The delicate droplets of water shimmered in the morning light, reminding Chipeta of tiny glass beads.

At the river, Chipeta stooped and dipped her basket into the frigid water. She noticed her surroundings as the water from the Arkansas River swirled into her container. Her eyes widened in surprise when she caught sight of a large beetle crawling along the bank. He carried a tiny droplet of dew upon his black shiny back.

Chipeta watched in wonder as the insect gradually lowered its front legs and head, leaving his tail end pointed skyward. Fascinated, Chipeta set her basket aside and knelt down on the ground. She continued to observe the creature as it carefully positioned itself. Slowly and steadily the small watery bead ran down the length of its dark hard shell and into the beetle's tiny jaws. Even the crawlers needed the life-giving waters of Mother Earth.

She put her basket into the swift current to finish filling it. Brown-and-white mud swallows darted back and forth over the moving water, calling to one another. Chipeta enjoyed their acrobatics as they dove up and down searching for flying insects. A nosy old trout rose to the surface of the water to investigate. The world was full of amazing things, and Chipeta was glad to be a part of it.

She pondered the lifeways of her people. They had survived in the wilderness for as long as they could remember. Creator had given all of his creatures wisdom that they might live abundantly and peacefully with each other in the natural world. Her people had learned to observe and appreciate the wild creatures that lived upon Mother Earth.

For centuries her people had followed the elk, deer, and mountain goats as they migrated from their wintering grounds into the Rocky Mountains. The animals had given them food, shelter, and wisdom about the lands they lived upon. By observing the animals, the Utes knew when they should move their camps. It had been that way ever since *Sinawaf* had made the Ute people.

Chipeta stopped to honor Creator. She thanked him for putting her people in the safety of the rugged mountains and valleys. She praised him for the water in the river and for the sweet air she breathed. Chipeta was grateful for the land and the fresh spring grasses that fattened their ponies.

The young woman whispered prayers for her husband and her beautiful son, too. Creator had indeed blessed her with abundance. He had given her someone to love and to care for. Chipeta rejoiced at the wonder of it all.

The snowcapped mountains of the San Juans stood majestically in the distance. Their rugged peaks towered high into the cloudless sky, tugging at Chipeta's heart and mind. She smiled to herself. It was time once again to return to their high alpine valleys and hilltops. The thought of the upcoming journey filled Chipeta with pleasure.

She slowly lifted her basket onto her hip. The heaviness of the basket slowed Chipeta down as she followed the trail along the riverside. She pushed the willow branches aside as she stepped over small puddles of water. The air had grown warm and dragonflies with their iridescent wings hovered over-head. Chipeta swatted at the mosquitoes and gnats that buzzed around her, and grimaced as she climbed the gravely bank.

Chipeta tried to think good thoughts as she struggled up the slope. She, Ouray, and Paron would be leaving for their summer grounds in a few days. They would be joining the rest of the Ute people in the mountains in the west. Soon the Bear Dance would be held, and everyone could celebrate the survival of another winter and the arrival of spring. Young men and women often found mates at the Bear Dance, too.

Thoughts of the celebration filled Chipeta with renewed vigor. She couldn't wait to see her friends and family, and to catch up on the latest news. She had much to share now that she was Ouray's wife and a mother.

It was in 1853, at the annual Bear Dance, Chipeta recalled, that Ouray met Black Mare. It was an important ritual that signaled the official arrival of spring and the awakening of *qwe auget*, the bear, after his long winter's sleep.

Everyone in the village was busy making food and preparing the dance floor. Chipeta tried to help by gathering sticks for the *avi qui up*, wooden fence. The area representing the bear den was swept clean, and walls surrounding the dance floor were created by stacking the boughs and branches along its perimeters. The spacious entryway faced the east. Bear, it was said, chose a cave where the sun shines during the day.

Chipeta and Black Mare had dressed in their finest buckskin clothes. The shirts, leggings, and dresses were adorned with elks' teeth, tiny seed beads, and porcupine-quill embroidery. The dreary tones of winter were replaced by a kaleidoscope of vivid colors.

When the people had gathered, single men and women shyly walked into the dance arena, while Chipeta and the other spectators watched from the other side of the wooden structure. Chipeta's eyes danced with excitement as the couples paired off.

Young men and women stood opposite each other and waited for the dance to begin. The slow, steady grating sound of the *moraches* (a notched stick that is rubbed with another stick) filled the air. The dance was under way! The hum of the wooden instruments symbolized the growling bear as it woke from its long winter's nap.

Chipeta could feel the pulse of the music deep inside of her. Her moccasined feet began to move up and down. The men and women on the dance floor slowly shuffled forward.

The tempo of the *moraches* increased as the people danced. Anticipation grew as the people sang songs of thankfulness and joy. When the dance was over, a warrior donning a bearskin moved around the dance floor growling and clawing at the dancers and spectators. The adults laughed at the young children who screamed in delight as they scrambled to get away from the bear man.

When the dancing was done, matchmaking and feasting complete, Ute hunting parties rode into the nearby mountains in search of fresh game. Spring hunts meant that the people would have fresh meat to eat. Chipeta smiled thoughtfully; Ouray had married Black Mare shortly after the Bear Dance.

The large Tabeguache family spent much of their time traveling along the Arkansas River and trekking between the southern parts of the San Juans to the central Rocky Mountains. Soon they would be on the trail again. Chipeta picked up her step. She was eager to get home.

Suddenly Chipeta stopped dead in her tracks. She held the water basket on her hip tightly and quickly stepped off of the path. She hid herself among some low-growing bushes along the riverbank. Chipeta's heart pounded in her ears and she tried to catch her breath. She quickly glanced around at her surroundings. *Kwum-ci'*, the foreign invaders, she whispered to herself.

The stranger stood several yards downstream from Chipeta. He had not noticed her. The intruder had a colorless face that was covered in a tangled mass of red hair. It grew around the man's mouth and down his chin.

Chipeta had seen men like him before. She vividly remembered the traders who had visited her camp when she was a young girl. The pale-faced men came often to trade with Ute men and women. Everyone gathered around the merchants, who brought strings of bright shiny beads, calico fabrics, wool blankets and shawls, and metal cooking utensils. The Utes provided the traders with fresh game and animals skins in exchange for their goods.

This man was different. He traveled alone, carrying a shovel and a strange metal pan. His bizarre actions fascinated Chipeta. The red-haired man waded out into the water with his shoes on. He dipped the large dish into the water and pulled it back out. The dish was filled with sand and gravel from the bottom of the river.

Chipeta watched as he rocked the pan back and forth until the water had run out of it. He squinted as he pushed his dirty fingers through gravel and silt at the bottom of his pan. The man muttered to himself as he threw the contents of the pan back into the water. Chipeta kept her eyes on him as he repeatedly filled his pan with water and gravel and dumped it out.

Memories of her recent visit with Ouray crept into Chipeta's mind. Goosebumps covered her arms and legs, making her shiver. Ouray had heard stories of the men who were coming by the thousands in search of a strange-looking metal called "gold." Miners he had called them. Chipeta quickly backed away from her hiding place. She quietly slipped past the man in the water. Her brain tried to grasp the situation. Was it possible that the rumors were true? Could there really be so many of the white people?

The mountains had always sheltered her people from invaders. Her people followed the long-established trails of their Ute ancestors into their private mountain sanctuaries. Now others did too. Chipeta quickly made her way back to the lodge. She needed to tell Ouray about the unwelcome intruder.

Chapter 6

CHAOS AND CONFLICT

THERE WAS URGENCY IN Ouray's motions as he loaded his pony with his parfleche and bedroll. Chipeta's hands shook as she handed him a skin filled with water and a leather sack stuffed with pemmican and dried jerky. Her eyes pleaded for Ouray to stay home.

Ouray tied his rifle, along with the water skin and the food pack, onto his horse. He turned to bid Chipeta good-bye. Paron sobbed and lifted his arms toward his father. Ouray lifted his boy off of the ground and tenderly tapped his lips with his finger. The boy quieted at the whispered promise that Ouray would take him hunting when he returned. Teary-eyed, Chipeta forced a smile. She needed to be strong for Paron, and for Ouray.

Her husband, she knew, needed to visit the Pikes Peak region and learn what he could about the miners and settlers who continued to move into the Colorado Territory. They had come from lands east of a mighty river called the "Mississippi." Ouray hoped to prevent a possible invasion and the possibility that the government would try to move the Tabeguache people.

Ouray's face had grown dark when Chipeta recounted her experience at the river. He rushed out of the lodge and immediately summoned Nevava and the other leaders. They gathered together to discuss the potentially explosive situation. The discovery of gold near Denver had been disastrous for their people.

Many of the miners had stayed east of the great snowy range. Now there was the possibility that the gold seekers would cross the boundaries and move into Ute territories. The news stirred the people in camp. Young braves talked of chasing them away and killing the men if necessary. Leaders agreed that they could deal with a few fortune seekers, but, if the rumors were true, the Utes would soon be outnumbered.

The Ute leaders could not understand how the foreigners could lay claim to their ancestral lands. *Sinawaf* himself had put the Ute people there long before the white men ever came.

Chipeta watched as Ouray set Paron down on the ground beside her. Her husband smiled as he touched her cheek with his calloused finger, wiping away her tears. He reminded Chipeta that the trip was necessary for the good of their people. She nodded hesitantly, knowing in her heart that Ouray was right. Through watery eyes, Chipeta watched as her husband mounted his horse and galloped away.

The trip, she knew, was a perilous one, and Chipeta trembled at the thought of losing him. Plains tribes had become more aggressive, attacking the settlers and miners who got in their way and any others who might threaten them. She couldn't imagine facing the future without her beloved friend and husband. Paron, too, needed his father. There was nothing Chipeta could do but wait.

Nearly a month after their tearful good-bye, Ouray rode back into camp. Chipeta and Paron hollered with joy as they ran across the ground toward Ouray. Exhausted and downtrodden, Ouray swiftly dismounted his horse and pulled Chipeta and Paron close to him. Chipeta rejoiced that her dearly loved husband had made it safely back home. She helped Ouray unload his pony, and together she, Ouray, and Paron walked back to their teepee. Chipeta knew by Ouray's expressions that the news he carried back from the Pikes Peak area was bleak.

She listened in horror as Ouray described the unruly conditions east of the Continental Divide. Tens of thousands of whites swarmed the mountains and plains. The intruders were breathing down the necks of the Ute people. It was just a matter of time before Ute lands were overrun.

The news shook Chipeta to the core. Her body shuddered and she pulled her shawl around her shoulders, as if to protect herself from Ouray's words. She could scarcely imagine the large masses of people living on the eastern prairies and in the foothills. Ouray's depressing news made it clear that frequent encounters with the miners and settlers would be unavoidable.

Chipeta and Ouray talked for hours about the current state of affairs. Congress had named the area east of the divide the Territory of Colorado. William Gilpin, who had been superintendent of the Conejos Agency, was appointed to be territorial governor.

Towns and cities made of wood and brick had been built all over the eastern plains. Thousands of soldiers rode their horses through the area in search of raiding tribes. Military forts had been built to protect the men, women, and children who lived in Ute hunting grounds. Chipeta brought her hands to her face as she listened in disbelief. What would become of their land? What would happen to the Tabeguache people?

Chipeta wished she had never seen the red-haired prospector. His presence in their valley had changed everything. She wished the miners would stay on the east side of the mountains so that her family could live in peace. The constant worries about the government agencies and the possibility of a rush of people into the mountains drained Chipeta of her energy.

Constant strife and disharmony among her people continued to take its toll. The Tabeguache had already moved their lodges, trying to avoid the soldiers and foreigners who lived in the southern part of their winter territories.

Chipeta realized that their homelands in the Arkansas Valley were threatened too. A dark and murky future rushed toward them like the raging river during snowmelt. The torrent of unstoppable intruders would sweep through the valleys and mountains, destroying everything near and dear to the Utes.

In the months that followed, thousands of miners poured into the hillsides and ripped Mother Earth open with their picks and axes. Their dreams of becoming rich overnight made them reckless. They left horrid gaping holes and mounds of yellow and gray ore all over the pristine hillsides.

Forests were demolished as the whites made wooden buildings and cities all over the land. Fences were put up to protect their claims and families from the natives who lived in the area. Rebellious Ute warriors quickly tore them down and threatened harm if the trespassers did not leave their lands. Battles ensued and both sides lost lives.

Chipeta and the other women and children stayed close to their camps. She did not allow Paron to wander very far. Her eyes constantly scouted the landscape as she traveled back and forth to the river, hunting for bulbs and berries. She carried her knife with her wherever she went.

Hunting territories, too, were disappearing at an alarming rate, and the game available was not enough. Chipeta hated the fact that so many people competed for the land's resources. The simple way of life she had known as a young girl was replaced by turmoil.

Raids on other tribes and white settlers were becoming everyday occurrences. The white men slaughtered buffalo by the thousands, leaving their carcasses to rot in the sun. When their buffalo were taken by the newcomers, the Utes were forced to rustle cattle from the settlers in order to feed their own families.

Frightened citizens demanded that the United States government do something to help them. Chipeta could not understand their reasoning. The Ute people tried hard to resolve their conflicts peacefully. Her people were outnumbered by the newcomers. For every Ute person, there were at least five of the non-natives. Chipeta realized that their numbers would only increase.

Chipeta was only six winters when the first treaty with the United States had been signed. Now the government planned to include the Tabeguache band as part of the Abiquiu Agency in New Mexico. Chipeta and Ouray both realized that their situation was about to worsen.

The process of putting many of the region's tribes onto reservations had already begun. Hundreds of Utes living in the Utah territory were placed under the government's supervision in 1861. Within a short amount of time, many of the Utes had perished due to disease and starvation. Conditions at the agency were deteriorating rapidly, leaving the Ute people to fend for themselves.

When food was not available, the hungry Utes raided the Overland Stage Company in Wyoming and westbound wagon trains. Government soldiers from Fort Halleck and from Col. John Chivington's new Colorado Infantry quickly pursued the Ute marauders. Hostilities grew out of control. The Utes resisted the idea of being controlled by the agency workers and soldiers.

Still the government persisted. New agencies were established at Abiquiu, Cimarron, Tierra Amarilla, New Mexico, and in Denver, Colorado. Chipeta listened in disbelief as details about the reservations were revealed. News of smallpox epidemics in the San Luis Valley sickened Chipeta, and she grew furious.

The Utes had never known diseases such as the white man's illnesses. The agencies seemed to harbor these kinds of illnesses. Chipeta's stomach turned at the thought of the men, women, and children whose bodies were covered in hideous pus-filled blisters. The infections had spread rapidly, claiming countless victims.

To make matters worse, starvation was another issue the Utes at the agency were facing. Because of their diminished hunting territories, they had become dependent upon the government's provisions to help them through the wintertime. Rations were late in coming and often arrived at the agency spoiled and full of worms and mold.

The thought of being forced to live there frightened Chipeta. She would do whatever it took to help Ouray maintain peace with the whites. Her husband's negotiating skills were valued by the government and by Ute leaders who did not understand English.

Chipeta listened attentively as Ouray translated the speeches of Ute leaders into Spanish, speeches that were then converted into English for the government officials. Ouray spent more and more time speaking on behalf of the Ute people. Thousands of Utes depended upon his ability to convey their messages to the government's representatives. The burden of their future lay upon Ouray and the other leaders' shoulders.

Chapter 7

HAPPINESS AND HEARTACHE

CHIPETA AND OURAY SAT SIDE BY side under a small stand of juniper trees. They talked about the disturbing turn of events in Utah. The Utes there worked hard to feed themselves. There was very little game to be found. The Mormon settlers had insisted that the Ute try their hands at farming, yet the land could not support the vegetation. Paron was almost six winters, and Chipeta and Ouray struggled to keep their family together throughout the difficulties facing their people.

The government had set up a small reservation near Denver for the Tabeguache people who still hunted buffalo on the eastern plains. Shortly after that, a permanent reservation was established in Conejos, in southern Colorado.

Chipeta, Ouray, and Paron settled in their childhood homelands. Ouray worked feverishly to assist government officials as they worked to solve the continued conflicts with the non-natives moving into the central Rockies.

Whenever an agreement was made, the men from Washington put the words onto paper. They asked Ouray and the other leaders to honor the agreement by putting their marks on the line at the bottom. The white men smiled as they added their own names to the paper.

With each new treaty, Chipeta felt more unsettled. She grew suspicious of the white man's language. Too many promises had been broken, and yet the men in Washington continued to create additional documents for her people to sign. With each new treaty came the reality of loss. The lands that Chipeta had known since birth were rapidly disappearing.

But for the moment, they were surrounded by peace, despite their dark thoughts. Paron ran barefooted along the banks of the river, skipping stones across the surface of the water. His brown, lean body had grown a great deal, and his long black hair lay loose about his neck and shoulders. The boy had many of his father's handsome features, and Chipeta was grateful that the boy was healthy.

She and Ouray watched as Paron tried to catch minnows. The child cupped his hands and slowly put them into the water. He waited. Suddenly, Paron pulled his hands out of the river, splattering himself with icy cold water. The boy gasped and let out a cry. He shivered and ran toward the warmth of his mother and father.

Chipeta promptly gathered Paron into her arms. She began to dry him off with a soft piece of doeskin. She teased the boy playfully for getting water and sand on their blankets. Paron looked up at her with his big brown eyes and smiled. Ouray reached over and gently tugged at the boy's long wet hair. Chipeta cherished this moment of privacy with her husband and young son.

After she dried Paron's body off, Chipeta picked up a small buckskin shirt and helped the boy pull it over his head. As she did this, she studied the jagged scar on Paron's right shoulder.

She remembered when Paron tried to ride Thunder Cloud, Ouray's prized war horse. Many men in the camp had tried unsuccessfully to ride the horse. Ouray delighted in the fact that nobody could stay on the animal's back for very long. So Paron decided that he too would attempt to ride the legendary horse.

He was not even five winters when he had climbed onto the back of the enormous animal. Thunder Cloud instantly took off, while Paron held on for dear life! The animal snorted, stomped, and whinnied as he tried to hurl the small boy off of his back.

Determined, Paron tightened his grip on the reins. Thunder Cloud ran in the direction of an old gnarled tree with dying branches. Paron's eyes grew large as the horse rushed up to the tree and galloped under the low-hanging limbs.

Paron screamed in agony. A jagged branch caught Paron in the right shoulder, knocking him to the ground. The boy lay on the ground and yelped in pain, as blood from his wounded shoulder ran down his chest. Ouray's horse had overpowered another rider.

Chipeta and Ouray gently chided their son for his foolish behavior. Yet Paron's courageous attempt to ride Ouray's horse had filled them with pride. Paron was already following in his father's footsteps. He was physically powerful, and Paron had proven he was bold-spirited and an excellent rider. These were desirable traits in a young man. Word spread throughout the camp about Paron's ride. He soon gained the nickname "Little Chief" because of his daring adventure.

And now, a year after Paron's legendary ride on Thunder Cloud, the young child had been invited by Ouray to take part in his first buffalo hunt. The Tabeguache band would ride north and east over towering mountain peaks, toward the Denver agency.

The excursion would be long and dangerous. The crowded conditions on the prairie and the unending flow of whites bred ongoing tensions between the different tribes in the region. Soldiers from the east continued to patrol in hopes of keeping the settlers and farmers safe.

Chipeta knew that the outing was necessary for the welfare of her people. They must have fresh buffalo meat for the long winter months. Paron too, she realized, must learn the ways of his father and grandfather. Someday he would have a family of his own to support. His early training to become a skilled hunter and warrior was crucial to the people's continued survival.

Day after day, Chipeta busied herself with ordinary household tasks as she waited for the return of her family. As the fresh kills arrived at camp, Chipeta and the other women prepared the hides for tanning. They scraped the fat and flesh off of the massive hides using a chiseled bone. When the hides had been scraped clean, the women stretched the skins out on the ground, pegging them down.

The hides were scrubbed with water and then wrung out. Once the skins were cleaned and rinsed, the women brought out containers filled with the brains of animals. They carefully applied the brains onto the hides with their bare hands. When the hides were completely covered they were left in the sun to dry. Then they would rinse the brains off of the hides and dry them out.

Chipeta also cut buffalo meat into strips to be smoked and dried. The entire camp kept busy in a flurry of activity. In the quiet of the evenings in front of the campfire, Chipeta spent her time adding beads onto leggings for Ouray. She made a series of triangular shapes on them. The shapes reminded

Chipeta of her mountain homelands. She tried hard to think good thoughts as Ouray and Paron traveled through the hostile territory.

It had been almost three weeks since the hunting party's departure from camp, and there had been no word. A restlessness settled upon Chipeta. She could not wait another day for Paron and Ouray to return. She desperately wanted to ride her horse eastward to find her husband and son.

Every day, Chipeta sat outside the front door of the lodge with her bead-work. She was relieved to think that she, Ouray, and Paron would soon be on their way back to Conejos. Chipeta picked up a tiny bead and threaded it onto her needle. She carefully added the white bead onto Ouray's leggings. Chipeta squinted in the afternoon light as her eyes scanned the horizon. The plains before her were empty, and there were no riders in the distance. She continued to wait outside her lodge, adding bead after bead to the buckskin leggings.

At last Chipeta heard the joyful cry. Ute riders could be seen in the distance moving toward camp. Chipeta jumped up, dropping her beads and the buckskin leggings. She was eager to be reunited with her family. She smiled as she ran through the encampment.

Chipeta and the other women made joyous tremolo with their tongues as the hunters rode into view. They shouted greetings as they crowded around the hunters. The pleasant moment ended abruptly, and for a moment no one spoke. Horses were loaded with plenty of fresh meat, yet the mood of the hunters was somber.

Three warriors had not returned. Ear-splitting screams broke the silence, as the dead men's families tore at their hair and clothes. Wives and children rushed forward, desperately searching for their loved ones. Chipeta's heart beat frantically as she hurried among the riders calling for her boy and for Ouray. Her legs could hardly carry her as she stumbled past the others.

Chipeta bellowed when she saw Ouray. His face was ashen and his expression grim. A sickening feeling came over her, and she shook her head in disbelief. She refused to believe that her son had not returned. Chipeta ran back and forth through the crowd screaming for Paron.

Ouray had dismounted his horse and stumbled toward his distraught wife.

She grabbed Ouray's arm and pulled at his shirt. Her eyes searched Ouray's wretched face for answers. Ouray slowly shook his head from side to side. Chipeta's legs collapsed under the weight of the news. Her only child was gone. Desolate and in shock, the husband and wife slowly shuffled across the encampment toward their lodge.

In the dark of night, Ouray wept as he told Chipeta about the attack. The two-week hunting trip had been a successful one. Both father and son had ridden their ponies across the vast grassy prairies. Paron had demonstrated many fine skills during the trip. Ouray was filled with pride as he watched his son participate in the hunt. He had waited for this moment and cherished this important milestone in Paron's life.

After the hunt there was plenty of buffalo to share with their families. Everyone in the hunting party was in a celebratory mood. It was time to return with their load of meat. They were eager to reunite with Chipeta and the others in the main camp. Paron was coming back as an accomplished hunter, and couldn't wait to tell his mother about his hunting adventure.

On the night before their return, the Ute camp was attacked. A large band of Sioux warriors had surprised the small hunting party. During the battle, three Utes were killed and dozens of ponies were taken. Ouray and the other Ute warriors boldly fought off their attackers. When the battle was over, Paron was nowhere to be found. The boy, it seemed, had been taken captive by the enemy.

Chipeta wanted to scream as Ouray described the details. She couldn't imagine someone else taking her boy. Would they kill him? Would Paron be traded to someone else for a horse? Would another Sioux woman raise her son? Chipeta and Ouray agonized over these terrifying unknowns.

Ouray focused his eyes on the flames of the cooking fire. He couldn't bear to look at his grieving wife. He continued to describe the horrifying days after the attack. He had searched in vain for his son and his captors. They were nowhere to be found.

Chipeta sobbed uncontrollably. The loss of Paron was more than she could bear. She took her knife out of its beaded scabbard. Her hands shook as she slashed at her long black hair once more. Her tears flowed freely down her face as she and Ouray slashed at their arms in mourning.

Chipeta's hands shook as she applied pine pitch onto her forehead. Her dreams of watching Paron grow into manhood had disintegrated like the wood branches in the fire pit. Chipeta slowly scooped their blackened remains out of the pit and rubbed them over her face.

Dazed and heartbroken, Chipeta and Ouray rode in silence as they slowly made their way to the western slopes. Chipeta could hardly move forward. Her body and heart ached from an unspeakable pain. She could not bear the thought of going home without her son. As the procession of Utes moved forward, Chipeta and Ouray lagged behind. Their eyes constantly scanned the eastern horizon hoping that Paron would somehow appear before their eyes. The physical and emotional wounds of Paron's disappearance would never go away.

CHIPETA WARMED HER HANDS over the crackling fire. It was late in the afternoon, and the weather was bitter. Icy cold winds howled down the gulches and

Chapter 8
BROKEN PROMISES

through the piñon trees, blasting at the sides of the lodge. The women chattered excitedly as they entered the teepee carrying bundles of skins. They had gathered to sew clothes, to bead, and to keep each other company while their husbands were in Washington, D.C.

Once everyone was settled among the thick buffalo robes, they quickly got to work on their projects. Chipeta and a few of the women worked on their finished skins, while others sewed beads onto buckskin clothing. They laughed and talked among themselves as they worked. Chipeta was glad for the fellowship, as her teepee had been lonely without Ouray.

Chipeta pulled her bone awl out of its pouch. She held it firmly in her hand and pushed its sharpened point through the thick leather. Chipeta grew envious as she listened to the women swap stories about their children. She wished that she was making new clothes for Paron. Instead, she worked on leggings for her loving husband, Ouray.

As she worked the awl, an image of Paron's beautiful brown face remained fixed in her mind. Oh how she missed his bright eyes and his intelligent questions. Chipeta's mind drifted away from the conversation. Her boy would have been eleven winters by now. Was it possible he was still alive? Did his new mother love him like she did? The last thought made her eyes well up with tears.

Chipeta silently glanced at the series of small scars on her arms. Paron's death had dazed her and she hardly felt the knife cut into her skin. Chipeta ran her slender finger over the raised blemish. Her physical wounds had healed, but her heart was still bleeding. She and Ouray would never get over losing Paron.

A sudden gust of wind rattled the leather covering of the lodge, pulling it away from its ties. Cold air rushed into the lodge, startling the women. Chipeta jumped up to fasten the ties. She shivered as she sat down in front of the fire on a buffalo robe. She put more cedar on the fire and picked up her sewing.

Talk in the teepee had turned to other matters now. The women's faces had grown serious as they begin to speak of the new government treaties. Chipeta's heart thudded in her chest as she thought of the leaders of all seven bands of Utes, including her husband, meeting in Washington, D.C., to discuss an agreement.

The women talked about their future with uncertainty. Once again, the Utes would be forced to give up more land. The new reservation would be placed somewhere near Cochetopa Creek, sixty miles north of Conejos. Chipeta's fingers felt useless as she tried to concentrate on her sewing. Her mind could not stay in once place. Thoughts of Conejos and her childhood flashed rapidly through her mind. She could see Ouray's tired and solemn face as they visited about his trip to the capital city.

Chipeta pitied her husband and the other leaders. They carried a heavy burden as they traveled to Washington, D.C., to negotiate on behalf of their Ute tribesmen. They had been let down by the government's meaningless agreements. The men in Washington did not keep their promises, yet they constantly looked for ways to take more land from the Utes.

Treaties disgusted Chipeta. They took Ouray far away from her, making her lonely and uneasy. She continually worried about her husband's well-being. Whites and Utes alike had criticized him as he worked vigorously to promote peace.

Chipeta and Ouray exchanged ideas as they took unhurried walks on the hillsides near the Conejos Agency. Privacy was rare, and Chipeta relished time alone with her husband. She listened as Ouray agonized over decisions, knowing that his mark on the treaty would continue to alter their traditional way of living.

Some in the Ute communities did not approve of the treaties, and Chipeta knew it. The women she visited with talked of these things. In their eyes, the papers the government had written were meaningless. They had not stopped the intruders. The Utes were greatly outnumbered by miners and settlers who continued to trespass onto their protected lands.

Still, Chipeta hoped that her husband's efforts would help the Utes avoid further conflicts. The possibility of an attack like the Sand Creek Massacre constantly stayed in her mind.

Chipeta ran her hand over the soft skin leggings in her lap. She only had a few more holes to punch. Her fingers quickly worked the awl in and out of the softened leather. Soon she would sew the pieces of the leggings together with some sinew. The women continued their conversations, but Chipeta hardly heard them.

She considered the fact that countless troops had been brought to Colorado to help maintain order. Forts had been set up all over the Colorado Territory to protect the miners and settlers, and to protect their appointed lands west of the mountains. The military men were well equipped with weapons and horses. What would stop them from attacking the Utes? she wondered.

Chipeta grew sick as she remembered the purposeless deaths of hundreds of Arapahoes and Cheyenne in the Colorado Territory in the month of November when the men hunted deer. She and Ouray were living in Conejos with their families.

Four winters had passed since the dreadful Sand Creek Massacre. Chipeta vividly recalled the day when panicked messengers from the east had reached the Tabeguache camp a month later. The Utes listened in horror as the men recounted the unprovoked assault on the Arapahoes and Cheyenne in haunting detail.

Their leader, Black Kettle, had agreed to live on lands assigned to his people by the United States government. Their band was camped along Sand Creek, in the eastern part of the Colorado Territory. As a gesture of peace and friendship, Black Kettle hung a white flag and an American flag over his teepee. He had put his faith in the government's treaties, believing that he and his people were safe from harm. This was not so.

During the quiet hours of dawn, Col. John Chivington and his troops ruthlessly attacked the encampment. There had been no warning. Hundreds of Arapaho and Cheyenne men, women, and children awakened to the terrifying sounds of bugles and cannons, and the shouts of the soldiers as they blasted their way through camp with their rifles and swords.

The village was surrounded, and there was no hope of escaping the soldier's brutality. Hundreds of women, children, and a handful of men were cruelly slaughtered by Chivington and his ruthless men. The treaties the Cheyenne and Arapaho leaders had signed with the government had not saved them. The news left Chipeta stunned and saddened. She shivered as she remembered the bearded man. Chivington had visited Conejos during the treaty talks five winters before.

Chivington and his troops had accompanied Governor Evans as he made his way to the San Luis Valley for a meeting with the Ute leaders. Chivington was ordered by Governor Evans to demonstrate a new and powerful weapon. The small cannon exploded with a flash and an enormous bang, terrifying the Utes who had gathered to watch.

In her mind, Chipeta could see the same horrified looks on the faces of the Arapahoes and Cheyenne as the cannons blew apart their lodges. What kind of men were they? They had killed innocent people, and the citizens of the Colorado Territory hailed them as heroes. It was only after the truth came out that Chivington was relieved of his duties, as was Governor Evans.

Five winters ago, a year before the deadly Sand Creek Massacre, Ouray and

Chipeta (front row, second from left) sits next to Ouray following the Brunot Treaty in 1873. (Courtesy of the Denver Public Library, Western History Collection, #X-30679)

the Tabeguache leaders had agreed to the Conejos Treaty. They said they would stay in the territories west of the Continental Divide and leave the miners and settlers to themselves. In exchange, the government promised to give the Tabeguache people at least 150 head of cattle every year for five years, and 1,000 head of sheep every year for the first two years.

Along with the livestock, the Tabeguache people would receive $10,000 a year in trade goods, and another $10,000 worth of food rations. The new agency would be furnished with a blacksmith, too. Ouray, along with nine other leaders, signed the agreement in hopes of keeping government soldiers away from their people. Satisfied with the new arrangements, Governor Evans gave seven of the men silver medals.

The Tabeguache people could not count on the government for trade goods or rations. The details of the treaty had been ignored, and the Utes were left to fend for themselves. Luckily for them, the game was plentiful at that time, and they would not have to depend upon the government's scanty rations.

Her childhood in Conejos had been a happy one, and Chipeta's heart and mind were filled with countless memories. She would always have the wisdom of Mother and Grandmother. Those were things that the government could not take from her.

In Washington, Ouray had addressed the council. "The agreement an Indian makes to a United States treaty is like the agreement a buffalo makes with his hunter when pierced with arrows. All he can do is lie down and give in," he said as he prepared to sign the new document.

On March 2, 1868, Ouray and other Ute leaders reluctantly put their names on the Hunt Treaty. The government declared that the western third of Colorado would belong to the Ute people forever.

Ute riders traveled north with officials to locate a place to live within the appointed boundaries, one of which was the Los Piños River. They came across a long, magnificent valley, nestled among the hills near Cochetopa Pass. The Los Piños River boundary did not exist there, yet Ute leaders refused to budge from the site.

Government representatives did not want to jeopardize the new agreement, so they named a small creek flowing through the area Los Piños Creek. The matter was settled, and the new Los Piños Agency was established. According to the treaty, the Utes would live there forever.

Instead of 23.5 million acres, Ute lands had dwindled to just over 15 million acres. The new pact also declared that the easterners would be kept out of the new Tabeguache territory, and government soldiers would be on hand to protect the Ute boundaries.

There was little excitement as Chipeta and the women took down their lodges. The mood of the camp was dark and gloomy. Chipeta packed her dried roots and plants, all of her beading, and the household items into her leather packs. When the long procession began to move, Chipeta's heart broke. She couldn't bear to say good-bye to the long-established lands of her family. She said little to Ouray as the Utes began their sixty-mile journey northward.

She had finally settled in at the Conejos Agency, only to move once more. Chipeta knew little of the new location and wondered if the land would sustain her people. For two long weeks the people traveled over a rocky landscape toward their destination.

Once again, Ute leaders had put their faith and futures into the hands of the white men. They signed the treaties, giving away more of their lands. The Utes settled in the northwestern part of the San Juan Mountains as miners, settlers, and ranchers rushed in to stake claims on the old Ute territories in the eastern sections.

Officials had promised to provide the Los Piños Agency with a school, a carpenter, a blacksmith, and a farmer, as well as a house for an agent. A government agent would be on hand at all times in case the Utes had any problems or complaints.

Although the Los Piños territory belonged to the Tabeguache Utes, the tiny print in the government's treaty stated that roads, highways, and railroads authorized by law would be allowed through the reservation.

Chapter 9
THE BRUNOT TREATY

CHIPETA AND OURAY SURVEYED THE surroundings of the new Los Piños Agency with dismay. They glanced nervously at one another and then at the agency buildings in progress. Timber for the agent's log cabin had been stripped off of a nearby hillside by agency carpenters. They hacked and sawed at the towering ponderosa pines until they had fallen. Chipeta stared at the stumps and piles of sawdust on the hill. She shook her head sadly as she silently apologized to Mother Earth.

The travois had been untied from the horses, and now it was time to set up the lodges. Chipeta and the other women quickly went to work setting up camp, while Ouray and the other men took care of the ponies and hunted for fresh meat.

While they lifted the tall pine lodge poles into place, Chipeta thought of the changes that had occurred. She despised the fact that intrusive agents and the workers lived at the agency too. She failed to understand why the government insisted that non-natives live on lands that were given to the Tabeguache Ute.

Once the teepees were constructed, Chipeta began sorting through parfleches and baskets on the ground. She carried them one by one into the teepee, putting each parcel in its appropriate place. At least she had the familiar and orderly surroundings of their lodge, she thought.

Chipeta picked up another pack, and as she did so, she looked toward the agent's cold, square house. She could not imagine living in such a structure, away from the familiar sights, smells, and sounds of Mother Earth. She had purposefully set up their lodge away from the agent's log cabin. She preferred the quiet sounds of the creek as it trickled across the meadow to the obnoxious manmade sounds of hammers and saws.

Weary and hungry, Chipeta took a moment to rest. She opened a small leather pouch and pulled out a piece of pemmican. She sat down in front of her lodge and nibbled at the tiny pieces of meat and fruit.

Suddenly a magpie appeared in front of her. He hopped along the ground, squawking at Chipeta. She threw the bird a bit of the pemmican and watched as he picked it up in his beak. The sight of the bird eased the pain she felt. Magpie had blessed her with happy memories of her life in the valleys and mountains close to Conejos.

Chipeta's eyes followed the black-and-white bird as it flew into the air toward the hills. She whispered a prayer of gratitude as the bird disappeared among the trees. The winged messenger had reminded Chipeta of the long-honored traditions of her Tabeguache people.

She looked at the flurry of activity around her. Agency workers continued to hack away at the trees, making lumber for more buildings. Teepees lay scattered throughout the valley. Smoke from cooking fires drifted up into the sky. Chipeta stood tall and proud, lifting her head up to the mountain tops. Her heart beat to the sounds of the hammers as the men pounded nails.

Her beautiful brown eyes misted as she looked out at the valley. The government may have taken away her old Ute homelands, but she was still a Ute woman and the wife of Ouray. She would maintain her traditional Ute way of living and honor her ancestors by living a good and noble life.

Just when it seemed that things were beginning to calm down, Chipeta and Ouray were caught off guard. In April 1873, their hopes of a peaceful life at the Los Piños Agency were unexpectedly dashed. To Chipeta's dismay, trespassing miners had discovered rich deposits of gold-bearing quartz and placer gold deep in the heart of the Utes' allotted lands. The news immediately set off a frenzied rush toward the western part of the Rockies and toward the Los Piños Agency.

Greedy prospectors screamed for justice. They did not think it was fair for the Utes to have the mineral-laden lands to themselves. The disgruntled miners demanded that they have rights to dig for gold inside the Los Piños lands.

The promise of untold riches made Edward M. McCook, the governor of the Colorado Territory, determined to see the Utes removed from the gold-filled hills. He had been appointed shortly after the 1868 treaty, and Chipeta held him in contempt. She knew he hated the Ute people and the other natives who lived in the region.

Governor McCook was a loud and obnoxious man. He wasted no time in belittling the Ute people. He told the citizens of the Colorado Territory that the Utes were lazy and irresponsible. The man was a rival, and he threatened the safety and well-being of every Ute person. It did not surprise Chipeta that the devious governor rallied on behalf of the miners.

During the legislative session in January of 1872, he strongly insisted that another treaty be made with the Utes. The governor reveled at the thought of getting rid of the Ute people, who stood in the way of the miners' and settlers' progress.

The commissioner of Indian Affairs, Felix Brunot, and his partner, Nathan Bishop, called for the removal of the Utes from their "protected" lands. The representatives declared that the small number of Utes living there did not need such an immense area. Ouray; the new Los Piños agent, Charles Adams; and a few other Ute leaders met with the governor in Denver to discuss the proposed treaties.

Leaders in Washington had also become sympathetic to the miners' cause. Even though the lands had been set aside for the Ute people, the men in Washington now sought all of the lands in the new Los Piños district.

President Ulysses S. Grant agreed that the miners should be able to work in Ute territories, but he would not fight a war for the lands. Instead, he proposed that they negotiate for rights to the land. Brunot and Bishop came to Los Piños and quickly began a series of discussions with Ouray and the other leaders of the Tabeguache people. They hoped to sway the Utes to sign the treaty. Ouray and the other Ute leaders disagreed. They would not sell any part of their lands.

In hopes of persuading the Utes to participate in the Brunot Treaty, President Grant invited Ouray to Washington, D.C., along with Washington, Captain Jack, Charles Adams, and a trader from Saguache named Otto Mears. He had been trading with the Utes for years and had become accustomed to their language and customs. The government hired Mears to act as an interpreter during the three-month excursion.

When Ouray returned, Chipeta rejoiced. Ouray had not signed the treaty, but further discussions were in the works. During their visit, Washington hosts had showed their Ute guests the massive steel warships loaded with soldiers in the eastern harbors. Chipeta tried to imagine a floating armory.

Her eyes grew large in disapproval when Ouray described the huge cannons poking out of the square holes along the sides of the ships. A signal had been given, and Ouray and the party watched as the massive guns were fired into the air. The powerful steel cannons belched thick black smoke as they hurled iron cannonballs far into the Atlantic Ocean. They landed with a massive splash and disappeared among the waves. The guns were much more powerful than the ones Colonel Chivington had, and it was obvious that the government's military forces were great. The guns would easily defeat the Ute people.

It was August, the time when everything was ripe. The blistering sun beat down upon the lands of the Los Piños Agency. Nearly 2,000 Utes had gathered for the council. They had been camping in the valley along Los Piños Creek since the end of July, waiting for the negotiations to begin. Their teepees were scattered across the landscape for as far as Chipeta's eyes could see. She visited with friends and family members while Ouray and the men held council.

Chipeta's eyes constantly scanned the horizon for Felix Brunot and his procession of officials. She could hardly stand the suspense. The Indian commissioner had promised to find Paron if Ouray would help them with treaty talks. Her husband had been reluctant. The treaties would be devastating to the Utes, yet she and Ouray desperately wanted to see their son again.

Both she and Ouray were anxious about being reunited with their lost son. Over and over, Chipeta imagined throwing her arms around Paron's body and welcoming him home. She could still see his beautiful smile as he rode off with Ouray just before his capture. So many years had passed, and Paron would be a changed young man. The thought made Chipeta fearful. She wondered if Paron would remember her or Ouray.

Chipeta's heart leapt to her throat as Brunot and his riders came into view. She glanced nervously at Ouray. Her husband stood up and crossed the grounds. Chipeta and Ouray waited impatiently for Brunot to dismount his horse. The agent approached Ouray and extended his hand.

Chipeta surveyed the long procession of soldiers, cooks, servants, and clerks in hopes of seeing her son. She suddenly felt sick to her stomach. The heartache she felt overpowered her, and she could not bear to look at Ouray. His face was ashen and racked with pain and grief. Paron was not among the riders.

Brunot had befriended Ouray and learned about Paron's capture. Now it was obvious he had taken advantage of Ouray's grief and love for his son to keep the treaty talks open. Chipeta was furious. She stood next to her husband as Brunot promised he would keep looking for Paron. His words were of little comfort to her. Chipeta's heart was full of sorrow for her husband as he tried to focus on the matters at hand.

She started to leave the group for the comfort of her lodge, but Ouray's hand pulled at her own. He looked at her with tired eyes, asking her to sit with him at the meeting. Chipeta stared at Ouray in disbelief. Ouray's eyes pleaded, and Chipeta could not refuse her husband's request.

Chipeta walked stiffly by Ouray's side as they approached the agency building. Men and women stopped in their tracks and watched as Chipeta followed Ouray and the delegates across the grounds. Chipeta's face was red from embarrassment. She struggled with the old beliefs of her people.

Women had always been considered inferior and when it came to important tribal matters, they did not sit at councils with the men. Their place was at home. She was Ouray's wife and helpmate. Now she was an ambassador for the Ute people. Chipeta's body shook as she took her place next to Ouray.

Felix Brunot, Charles Adams, Otto Mears, and others present gave one another puzzled, disapproving glances. They were taken aback by Chipeta's bold move. Chipeta stared straight ahead, ignoring their reactions and whispers. She remained steadfast. She would not leave Ouray's side.

Chipeta stared at the ground as men began their negotiations. She watched as the men passed the pipe around. Its smoke filled the air with the sweet smell of tobacco. As the smoke rose, Chipeta whispered a prayer for her husband and for her people. She prayed that Creator would help her people during these difficult days.

Even in the scorching heat of the summer, the men wore their dark cloth suits, buttoning them from top to bottom. Chipeta stared at the black silk ties around their necks. They looked uncomfortable to Chipeta. Many of the men wore hair on their faces, hiding their mouths while they talked.

All eyes turned to Ouray. Chipeta watched as he began to address the men sitting across from him. Ouray's face was haggard. The strain of the endless disputes and negotiations were beginning to show their effects on her husband. She held her clenched hands in her lap while the officials finished their wordy speeches.

Chipeta was tired of the talking. She wished that she could go away from the meeting. She fought the urge to jump up and scream at the men gathered around them. She wanted the men from Washington to know that the Utes had done everything they could to cooperate with the easterners.

The men had forgotten the kind deeds of the Utes when the whites were lost on their lands and saved by her people. Chipeta stayed silent, knowing her words would be useless. The meeting was a formality, as the decision had been made the instant the gold had been discovered. There was very little the Utes could do.

One month later, on September 6, another council was held. Ouray, Chipeta, and many of the Ute leaders met with the government representatives again. The new treaties contained details of surveys done on the Los Piños lands.

Chipeta strained to understand the words that the officials used. Words such as "longitude" and "latitude" were used to describe their territory. Chipeta did not know their meanings. Surveyors had created invisible boundaries with their compasses and chains, and the government's method of determining borders baffled the Utes. For centuries their boundaries had been defined by age-old rivers and mountain ridges.

At end of the discussions, Ouray was offered a $1,000 a month salary and 160 acres of land along the bottomlands of the Uncompahgre River on the western slope of the Rocky Mountains. He and the Ute leaders accepted the treaty on the basis that they be allowed to visit the area in question. They wanted to see for themselves the actual lands being considered for the treaty. The Utes did not trust the government's new boundaries.

Ouray's dark eyes met Chipeta's for a moment. She knew that Ouray struggled under the weight of the decisions before him. Chipeta could hardly stand to see Ouray put his name on another treaty. It seemed that with every signature, a part of Ouray's spirit diminished.

On September 13, 1873, Ouray and seven Ute leaders signed the Brunot documents. The Ute delegates had not fully realized the true meaning of the contract. They believed they had only sold rights to the mines. Unfortunately, the agreement included most of the Ute lands, except for the small parcel of land in the Uncompahgre and Yampa Valleys.

The government had purchased the mineral-rich lands surrounding the Los Piños Agency from the Ute nation for 13 cents per acre. In turn, the administrators quickly sold the land to businessmen and settlers for $1.25 per acre. The amount the government had received for Ute properties was almost ten times the amount they paid to the Ute people.

A month after the treaty, Brunot contacted Ouray. He said he had located a boy named Friday who was said to be Paron. Chipeta felt mixed emotions as she and Ouray met briefly with the boy. She was hopeful that the boy would recognize her and Ouray, and that he would remember them.

Chipeta stood close to Ouray as he talked to the boy. He had been taken by the Arapaho when he was young, he told them. Chipeta's heart and mind were flooded with emotion. She held her breath as Ouray continued to assess him. Chipeta wanted desperately to believe that the boy was theirs. She was thirty winters and she had no children of her own. Chipeta had loved Paron like her own child, and she longed to sew for him and to watch him grow into manhood.

The young man eyed Chipeta and Ouray coldly. His rigid body stood at a distance from the couple and he looked as though he might bolt at any minute. For a while he said nothing. Then he spoke crushing words. The boy said he hated the Utes and that he did not want to live with them.

Disillusioned, Ouray declared that the boy was not his and he walked away. Chipeta put her hand over her mouth to stifle a scream. The pain of Paron's kidnapping was new all over again. Chipeta and Ouray grieved once more for the loss of their son.

Chapter 10

CAUGHT BETWEEN TWO WORLDS

IT WAS SEPTEMBER, THE TIME when everything gets yellow. The hills were ablaze with the colors of fall. The crimson leaves of scrub oak and the brilliant gold colors of the aspens took Chipeta's breath away. She halted her horse for a moment to take in the sight. A light breeze rippled through the gold- and copper-colored grasses in the fields. Chipeta closed her eyes and gave thanks to Creator. The sights and sounds of the morning had rekindled her spirit. For a brief instant, she was able to forget about the miserable months that followed after Ouray and the other Ute leaders signed the devastating Brunot Treaty.

Once again, the Ute people were homeless and moving over trails to unfamiliar lands. Chipeta felt the butterflies in her stomach when she thought of the new life she faced. Chipeta knew that the Brunot Treaty had altered the course of Ute history forever. She and Ouray had talked for hours about their impending move to the Uncompahgre Valley. Desperate times called for desperate measures, and the couple decided that they would give in to the government's expectations and live in a house at the agency.

Chipeta's pulse quickened at the thought of giving up the comforts of her teepee for the confinement of a house. Yet, in order to stay in the Uncompahgre Valley, she and Ouray realized that they needed to satisfy the government with their new lifestyle. They would settle down to farm and raise sheep as the whites had suggested. They would abide by the white man's laws, hopefully keeping what little land they possessed.

For centuries, the Utes had learned to adjust to the ever-changing climates of the Rocky Mountains. They had always been resourceful and cunning, and always managed to make the best of unpredictable situations. Now the Utes faced a challenge unlike any other. Their foe was not the inclement weather or the lack of game, it was the easterners who had overwhelmed them, taking away their territorial lands. Centuries of Ute customs and traditions lay in a delicate balance as they faced constant pressure from the government to conform to a non-native's life.

When the long procession of people reached the Uncompahgre Valley, their spirits were renewed. Chipeta's heart leapt at the view. The magnificent valley was surrounded by low, rolling hills and snowcapped mountains. The Uncompahgre River flowed slowly across the land, leaving rich, fertile bottomlands along its banks. The land to the east reminded Chipeta of the desert lands in her old homelands near Conejos.

The familiar sight of yucca and prickly pear filled Chipeta with a sense of hope. She was thrilled at the thought of riding into the high country in the summer. Perhaps their new homelands would serve the Tabeguache well.

Once they settled upon their 160-acre parcel of land given to them by the government, Chipeta and Ouray quickly began the process of building their home. Ouray's early experiences working for the Spanish ranchers had given him the necessary skills he needed to get the job done. In addition, Ouray hired Mexican laborers to help him. They mixed soil, straw, and water in a large trough. The thickened mud was shaped into bricks by hand and left in the sun to dry, then stacked one upon the other creating the walls of their home.

Before long, Ouray and his workers had completed the two-room house just west of the Uncompahgre River. He added a small adobe fireplace in the corner of their parlor to keep them warm during the cold winter months.

As with the cabin at the Los Piños Agency, Chipeta disliked the confinement of the four-sided dwelling. She felt as though she were disconnected from Mother Earth. She could not feel the cool breezes at night, and she missed the cozy times she and Ouray had talking by the campfire light.

Chipeta stood in the parlor, gazing at the busy floral pattern of their new carpet. She bent over and rubbed her hand across its woolly surface. The rug's fibers felt stiff and scratchy, and they could not compare to the soft, plush fur of her buffalo robes. Chipeta's eyes shifted to the overstuffed chairs and massive oak table in the parlor. Ouray's new government salary allowed them to purchase the household furnishings from stores in the Colorado Territory.

Unwanted thoughts of the past haunted Chipeta. She tried to shut them out of her mind, but she could not. She longed for the early days when she and Ouray lived off of the land. They had lived a simple and abundant life. Many of the things in her teepee had come from Mother Earth and the creatures that lived upon her. Blankets, teepee coverings, clothing, food, water skins, and utensils were all gifts from Creator. He had provided them with everything they needed to survive.

Silver-plated teapots and porcelain had replaced her willow baskets and wooden bowls. Instead of horn cups and spoons, she and Ouray drank from transparent glasses and they ate off of fine china using the peculiar metal silverware. Instead of a warm buffalo robe, she and Ouray slept on a shiny brass bed, which stood high off the floor.

Chipeta ran her finger along the wooden back of the rocking chair that was given to her. She shook her head as she studied its strange design. She recalled the first time she sat on the rocker. She was startled at its sudden motion when she grasped the arms of the rocker and pushed back with her feet.

Coupled with the displeasure of her new home, Chipeta's days were filled with new concerns. There were dishes to wash, silver to shine, laundry to do, beds to make, and cooking to be done over a hot wood-burning stove. Chipeta looked around the room through teary eyes. Everything around her seemed cold and lifeless, and they were all reminders that she and Ouray now lived their lives for someone else's sake.

Yet, in the midst of her non-native lifestyle, Chipeta still preserved the traditional skills she had learned as a girl. She continued to tan hides, gather and harvest plants, and do striking beadwork. They gave Chipeta great pleasure. These were things she would never leave behind.

Trying to stay focused, Ouray stayed busy with the issues the Tabeguache faced as a result of the new treaty. He continued to travel on behalf of the Ute people, and he continued to oversee the building of his farm. Mexican laborers planted crops and dug irrigation ditches across the property. Hayfields and gardens were cultivated. Adobe warehouses, barns, a root cellar, a privy, and corals were also built, adding to the value of their property.

For a time, Ouray, too, had adapted to some of the white ways. He wore a broadcloth suit, black leather boots, and a derby on his head. He acquired a fancy desk and chair, and carried calling cards with him when he visited people. Ouray loved riding in his fine-looking carriage, given to him by Governor Edward McCook. Although Ouray did not drink alcohol, he treated his guests to fine wine. Visitors found the couple's hospitality delightful.

Chipeta spoke very little English, unlike Ouray. The white man's words felt strange upon her tongue. She smiled and nodded at her guests, gesturing for them to come into their home. Chipeta's fluent Spanish allowed her to talk freely with her company who knew the language.

Visitors were amazed at Chipeta's ability to sing and play guitar. A reporter for the City of Ouray, William Saunders, recalled one of his experiences as he visited Chipeta and Ouray at their farm.

"Chipeta got used to my presence very soon, and gave free rein to her natural vivacity, talking Spanish, mostly about two pets she had, a mountain lion and a deer, which she had trained to consort with each other on most friendly terms. Her voice was low and clear and melodious and she talked with a fascinating play of features and gestures. ...

(Chipeta) rode like an Amazon and she and (her) horse might have been one, so perfectly did her body meet the movements of his. Her horse was a sorrel, a pony she told me she had raised herself, and he was that unusual horse, a natural single footer."

Even though Chipeta and Ouray had gained the admiration of well-known leaders and their wives, the couple still faced criticism from other government officials and the Utes. Chipeta felt as though she and Ouray were caught between two worlds—the traditional Ute way of living and that of a white society.

She and Ouray had sacrificed their customary way of life in an attempt to help their tribesmen and -women. She grieved the fact that they no longer lived in their customary tepee, nor did they ride their ponies across the eastern prairies to hunt buffalo. The couple had altered their old ways into a world of modern conveniences.

Within three years, Chipeta and Ouray had more than 100 acres of bottom-land fenced and plowed. Ouray's horse herd had grown to several hundred horses, and he owned thousands of sheep, in addition to some goats. He was one of the wealthiest men at the Los Piños Agency II. The Ouray Farms were the envy of numerous people, and Ouray's achievements as a farmer soon became an issue for many.

The Utes and whites alike told the couple that they were shaming their ancestors. Chipeta was sick at heart over their comments. She and Ouray had only wanted to help their people, yet many of their tribesmen and -women thought they were showing off. Chipeta had tried to reason with them. She grew frustrated over their attitudes. Didn't they know that the changes were necessary if they wanted to stay in the Uncompahgre Valley?

Chipeta wished she could escape the ugliness of their situation. The lives of the Utes had been turned upside down. Not only had they lost the home-lands that were near and dear to them, the Ute people in the territory of Utah were facing dire circumstances. Family members who had visited their relations at the Uintah Reservation in Utah had returned with sorrowful news. The Ute communities there were dwindling rapidly. Typhoid, smallpox, starvation, and violence had taken many lives.

The troubling reports exasperated Chipeta. Her heart ached for justice and at the same time she felt a stab of guilt as she and Ouray continued to reside at the farm. They did not lack for anything, while some of their people struggled to exist. She and Ouray had even taken in four young children to keep them from the dreadful life on the reservation.

Chipeta was increasingly resentful of growing criticisms that she and Ouray faced. Senator Henry Teller from the Territory of Colorado had enraged her with his anti-Ute statement. His words were like poison.

"Other anti-Utes declared that the perfidious [traitorous] Ouray had sold out his people for a thousand-dollar salary and one hundred and six acres of land. And the 'greedy redskin' had the nerve to set up a farm! He ought to be hustled on a rail back into the Elk Mountains for taking food out of white men's mouths by trying to earn a white man's living!"

The good deeds of the Ute people had already been forgotten, she thought. The senator did not appreciate the fact that he lived on lands once owned by the Utes. Differences between the two cultures and the devastating details of the Utah reservation were beginning to take its toll.

Ouray was growing weary of his leadership role. His relationship with some of the Utes had soured. Some of the young braves had even threatened to kill him. Chipeta felt a foreboding when she looked at Ouray. Her husband's eyes were dim, and his energy and his spirit seemed depleted. The real costs of the treaty could not have been measured. The white man's money and way of life was not enough for the pain they endured.

Chapter 11

A WOMAN OF COURAGE

WIDE-EYED IN TERROR, CHIPETA ran straight for the blacksmith's shop. Her heart pounded wildly as Sapavanero thrust himself at Ouray. With axe in hand, Chipeta's older brother lunged at Ouray. His rage-filled eyes stared in disbelief. He had missed his target. He swung wildly at Chipeta's husband again. All of a sudden Ouray ducked behind a post, just as Sapavanero swung the axe. Its sharp blade bit deep into the wooden beam.

Ouray's eyes were full of fury as he threw himself at Sapavanero and they rolled into a nearby ditch. Chipeta screamed, feeling as though her legs would buckle at any moment. She stared in disbelief as Ouray pulled his hunting knife out of its beaded sheath, bringing it to Sapavanero's throat. Her brother was about to die at the hands of her enraged husband.

Chipeta's heart beat frantically as she hurried toward Ouray. She pleaded for him to stop. Chipeta yanked the knife from his hands and threw it to the ground. Her legs buckled and Chipeta fell on her knees and wept. The struggle had strained every one of her nerves. There had been too much bloodshed already! Ever since the Brunot Treaty, Ouray's life had been in peril.

Chipeta could not bear to see her brother or her husband suffer. She loved both men dearly. Relieved, she held on to her brother and sobbed. Chipeta had saved him from certain death. It had not surprised Chipeta that her brother, Ouray's second leader in command, had attempted to end Ouray's life.

Her husband had once been highly respected, and now many of the men in the Tabeguache community and in the other Ute bands had grown hostile toward him. They did not support Ouray's decisions to sign the treaties or live the white lifestyle.

Chipeta understood why the people resented the government's worthless agreements. She detested them too. Millions of acres of Ute lands had vanished when the leaders had put their marks on the treaties. Rumors about Ouray's conspiracy with the United States government burdened her. Some of the Utes thought Ouray had given away their lands in exchange for his generous salary and the prime piece of land he lived on. In addition, Ouray had been assigned to be "chief" of the entire Tabeguache community, and this infuriated many.

At least today, the plot to kill Ouray had failed. Sapavanero and four other young braves had waited for Ouray at the Los Piños Agency II blacksmith's shop. They knew he had planned to have his horse shod. When Ouray had arrived with his horse, the blacksmith had given him a telltale nod. Instantly Ouray understood that someone waited for him in the shadows.

Chipeta was heartsick. She couldn't get over the fact that her brother had attempted to murder her husband. Both men had shamed themselves in front of her. Chipeta thought of her bold attempt to take Ouray's knife. She had even lectured her brother and her husband, both Ute leaders. Ouray and Sapavanero stood next to each other while Chipeta scolded them. Chipeta pleaded for them both to stop the violence. She looked at the men with a sorrowful expression. Each time someone died, a part of her died too. She felt as though she were caught in a trap. She could never allow anything to happen to her brother Sapavanero, but she would never betray the man she loved either.

At Chipeta's insistence, Sapavanero continued to work closely with Ouray. He had promised his sister and her husband that he would not attempt to overthrow Ouray again. Chipeta had saved his life, and Sapavanero knew he must regain Ouray's trust. Chipeta's plea had been heard and acknowledged. The men had forgiven each other, and soon Ouray had faith in his brother-in-law. Sapavanero was left in charge of the agency whenever Ouray was away hunting or on tribal business.

Despite the assassination attempt, Ouray still encouraged the Ute people to live peacefully with the non-natives. He expected his people to uphold the rules and regulations of the government's ever-changing treaties. Whenever someone from the Ute bands broke the rules and disgraced the Ute nation, Ouray was quick to punish them.

Chipeta's love for her husband kept her watchful at all times. She constantly obsessed about Ouray's safety, as many of the Ute men were still angry that the government had appointed him chief. Soon after the incident with Sapavanero,

Ouray hired Mexican bodyguards to watch over him and his wife. He had established a "secret police" to keep him informed of impending troubles.

Sadly, Ouray's troubles continued to plague him. Just four winters after the attempted murder, Chipeta's strong and fearless husband had become seriously ill. Fatigue, nausea, an aching back, and sore feet overwhelmed him. Chipeta felt an impending doom as she and Ouray rode their horses through the San Juan valleys eastward toward Cañon City. They had planned to visit the town's doctor.

Ute medicine men had not been able to end the pain, and Ouray's condition worsened. The kinnikinnick tea she had made for his kidneys had not helped him. She hoped that the doctor would be able to cure her ailing husband.

Chipeta could not understand the doctor's English, but the look on his face as he talked to Ouray did not lie. She glanced at Ouray with questioning eyes. Chipeta grieved as Ouray related the doctor's details to her. His condition was hopeless. Chipeta struggled to believe Ouray's words. He was suffering

Ouray and Chipeta pose in Washington, D.C. Ouray was critically ill when this picture was taken. (Courtesy of the Denver Public Library, Western History Collection, #X-30600)

from chronic nephritis. His kidneys were inflamed and would ultimately fail, resulting in death.

Stunned, Chipeta and Ouray rode back to the Los Piños Agency II in silence. It was clear that Ouray's misery was only beginning. Chipeta felt a hollow place deep inside of her. She had already begun to grieve. The thought of her husband's decline was unthinkable.

As Ouray's health worsened, Chipeta stayed close by his side. The legendary Ute leader was disheartened and exhausted. The once vibrant warrior slept constantly, while his guards sat outside his bedroom door. Despite his condition, he was still under the threat of an assassination.

One day, while Chipeta was looking out the kitchen window at the surrounding scenery, she caught a glimpse of a lone rider in the distance. Ouray's secret police had informed them earlier that a young Ute man by the name of Hot Stuff was on his way to seek revenge.

Because of the treaties that Ouray and the other Ute leaders had signed, Hot Stuff and his family had been forced onto a reservation. In addition to the appalling conditions there, overzealous missionaries had come to the reservation to take children away from their parents in hopes of saving their souls.

Hot Stuff too had been taken away from his relatives. The missionaries had forced him to go to the Carlisle Indian School. While he was there, Hot Stuff's cherished Ute heritage was taken away from him. Resentment toward his unnatural lifestyle at Carlisle remained buried deep inside of him. For months, Hot Stuff planned his vengeance. He rode his pony toward the Los Piños Agency II to murder the man he thought was responsible for his demoralizing past.

Chipeta studied Hot Stuff as he rode his calico pony across their property. The young man sat high and proud on his pony. He looked as though he was nearly eighteen winters. Chipeta warned Ouray of his approach.

Together the couple waited in silence as Hot Stuff came closer. When the rider was in weapon range, Ouray quickly fired at Hot Stuff, shooting him through the neck. Hot Stuff was dead, and Ouray was safe once more. Ouray stumbled back to the house. His face was a ghastly pale color, and the shooting seemed to drain him of his remaining energy.

As Ouray's bodyguards carried Hot Stuff's body away, Chipeta was flooded with a surge of emotions. On one hand, she was grateful for her husband's safety, yet she was dismayed at the death of another Ute man.

Chipeta reviled the missionaries who continued to trespass onto the reservations, snatching Ute children from their families in order to transform them into "civilized" people. The buckskin clothes their mothers had made them were removed and destroyed. Girls and boys wore the stiff shoes and "white" kinds of clothing and hairstyles.

Ute children were discouraged to talk of their families or their old way of life. It sickened Chipeta to think of the children living among strangers, away from their mothers and fathers. She ached when she thought of the terrified children crying for their families. Chipeta silently prayed that the Tabeguache people would not meet the same fate. She buried her head in her hands and cried for all of her people.

Chapter 12

THE MEEKER INCIDENT

CHIPETA QUICKLY MADE HER WAY across the parlor floor. Someone knocked deafeningly upon the wooden door of her home. It was late in the afternoon, and Chipeta had not been expecting company. The frantic pounding had startled her, and she cautiously opened the door and peered out. Two breathless riders from the White River Agency stood side by side in front of her. Chipeta promptly bid them in.

The men glanced nervously at one another and then at Chipeta. They asked to see Ouray, but he was out. Chipeta begin to grow tense. The tones of their voices told her that the matter was urgent, so she encouraged them to tell her what was going on.

Chipeta could hardly believe it, the White River agent, Nathan Meeker, was dead. He had been attacked and killed by a small band of White River Utes.

Chipeta remembered the reports from the White River Ute leaders when Agent Meeker had come to the White River Agency. He had traveled west from the Colorado Territory shortly after the treaty in November of 1878. The White River Utes had given up more of their land due to pressures from the government and miners. They had agreed to settle in the Yampa Valley, more than 150 miles north of the Los Piños Agency.

Meeker had plans to turn the unruly Utes into farmers and "civilized" people. Chipeta recalled the way in which the agent had treated the Utes. He had belittled the people, calling them "lazy savages." The sixty-year-old man had even requested that the Utes call him "Father Meeker." Neither she nor Ouray could understand his reasoning.

The White River Utes refused to bow down to the white agent, but they did not want to suffer the same fate as their friends and family on the Uintah Reservation. After toiling under the hot Utah sun, the farming had not been successful. The lack of water could not sustain the crops the Utes had planted.

The people faced disease and starvation.

Chipeta sat down on one of the overstuffed chairs. Her heart broke as the men continued their account. Meeker had persisted, moving the agency a few miles away, where there were lush green meadows and water nearby. He pressed down upon Chief Douglass and the White River Utes, commanding them to plow up the fields. Chipeta could scarcely believe that Meeker would hold back government rations from the hungry people in an effort to force them to comply with his wishes.

Douglass, Jack, and Jim Johnson had grown frustrated over Meeker's constant demands. The old man did not understand that the pastures were important to the people. Hundreds of horses grazed on the lush green grasses, and the Utes raced their ponies in the wide-open meadows. Meeker did not acknowledge the value the Utes placed on their horses. He had enraged Johnson with his request to plow up the field. Johnson himself had nearly a hundred horses that grazed upon the land.

On September 29, 1879, Meeker ordered agency workers to plow up the pastures. He had pushed the White River leaders over the edge by his tactless actions. Johnson became infuriated. He marched up to Meeker and pushed him down.

A panic-stricken Meeker wrote to the current governor of Colorado, Frederick Pitkin, asking for aid. He declared that the White River Utes were beginning to rise against the white people living at the agency. Meeker feared for his life and for that of his friends and family. Meeker's demand for help was fulfilled. Soldiers were soon on the way to the White River Agency.

Ute leaders had grown more and more cautious as they remembered the appalling tales of the Sand Creek Massacre. If the government's soldiers could take the lives of so many at the Sand Creek site, what would stop them from coming onto lands set aside for them by the treaties? Would their families be next?

The messengers continued to paint a grim picture. Within hours, nearly two hundred Ute men had gathered in Coal Creek Canyon north of the agency in an effort to protect their families and diminishing homelands.

Some of the warriors wore black and yellow war paint on their faces.

Tensions built as the Utes prepared for a possible battle. Some of the Utes rode horses, while others traveled on foot. Many of of them were well armed. They would defend their rightful territories at any cost.

Two Ute chiefs, Jack and Colorow, as well as Wilmer Eskridge, an ambassador from the White River Agency, rode toward the northeast in hopes of intercepting the soldiers. Maj. Thomas Thornburgh and his 178 troops had departed from Fort Fred Steele, Wyoming, two days earlier. When Thornburgh and his men were within forty-five miles of the reservation, they were approached by Jack and Colorow.

Jack reminded Major Thornburgh that the soldiers would be trespassing on their legal lands. He asked the major to abandon his plans.

Even though Jack had warned the major twice, the self-assured officer had ignored their warnings. He and his men continued to ride through the valley and within the reservation's boundaries along Milk Creek, just fifteen miles north of the White River Agency.

White River warriors rode toward the soldiers in an effort to protect their homes and families. Within minutes a bloody battle ensued. The major and his top-ranking officers were killed. Just hours after the attack on Major Thornburgh, Nathan Meeker and three other men at the agency were killed by a small band of Utes.

Meeker's wife, Arvilla, his daughter Josephine, Mrs. Shadrach Price—the agency farmer's wife—and her two young children had been taken captive. As Chipeta listened, her face drained of color, and she began to shake. It sounded as though things at the White River Agency were dangerously out of control. The last thought raced through Chipeta's mind, causing her to take immediate action. She sent a runner to find Ouray.

When her husband returned to the Los Piños Agency, couriers informed Ouray and the other Ute leaders that Col. Wesley Merritt was making his way to the White River Agency with 550 cavalry. Chipeta recalled the buffalo soldiers. She had seen the men with the dark skin and the woolly hair before when they visited Fort Garland a few years before the Brunot Treaty. Her people had called them the buffalo soldiers.

An enormous battle between the Utes and the soldiers was close at hand and the thought of it terrified Chipeta. She sobbed as she thought of the gruesome attack on Meeker. Poor Arvilla Meeker had watched in unspeakable horror as her husband was killed and his body mutilated.

This was the disaster the Utes had hoped to avoid. Thornburgh and his men had been killed, and the citizens of Colorado were in a panic, fearing for their own lives. Newspapers across the country published stories of the Meeker incident. They called for justice on behalf of the men killed at the agency and for the soldiers who had died during the battle near Milk Creek.

Chipeta and Ouray talked late into the evening about the unsteady circumstances. His faith in the whites had been shaken badly. The lands they had settled on had been invaded by miners, settlers, and soldiers. Now the citizens who had clamored for their land through the treaties screamed for their removal. Why should the Utes help now?

Ouray's words hit a nerve in Chipeta. She too, was perplexed by the attitude of the non-natives. Emotions of anger and resentment toward the outsiders who had treaded upon their land forced their way into her troubled mind. Meeker's self-seeking ideals had been his downfall. His actions had crushed the hopes of the Ute people—it was very likely that they would be forced to leave Colorado now.

Chipeta looked deep into Ouray's dark eyes. Fatigue and chronic pain had hardened his face, and deep creases lined his brow. His jaw and fists were clenched in anger and sorrow. Chipeta put her hand on Ouray's arm as she spoke. She reminded Ouray that Arvilla and Josephine Meeker had been kind to the Utes, and that they should not be held accountable for Meeker's foolish actions. She asked Ouray to send representatives to help rescue the Meeker captives before it was too late. If the Meeker women were harmed, the Utes would face even further devastating consequences.

To her relief, Ouray reluctantly agreed to Chipeta's requests. Too exhausted and ill to make the journey himself, Ouray sent for Sapavanero and Charles Adams, the Los Piños Agency II agent, asking them to go to the

White River Agency to negotiate for the captives' release.

Over the next several days, Chipeta's thoughts turned inward as she waited for the group to return. Chipeta fervently hoped that the men would be victorious in their efforts to free the Meeker captives. She paused for a moment and sent prayers to Creator. She asked him to protect them and to watch over her people.

Chipeta kept a constant vigil at the windows. Then finally the bedraggled group miraculously rode into view, alongside the Meeker captives. Chipeta rushed toward the women. She grasped their arms and pulled them into the safety of her home. Arvilla, Josephine, and Mrs. Price were overcome with emotion. After a grueling six-day ride, the exhausted and traumatized women and children shed tears of relief at the sight of the warm and cozy parlor.

The women were comforted by the familiar sights of the furnishings. Mrs. Meeker sat in the rocking chair, while the other women sat in the overstuffed chairs. Chipeta's young wards shyly gathered around their guests. Chipeta heated water for tea, while Ouray talked with Sapavanero and Charles Adams.

At dinner the women talked quietly among themselves. Chipeta caught glimpses of their conversations, yet couldn't understand the things they said. Words were not necessary, she thought. She knew that the hostages had been through difficult and frightening times. The look on Mrs. Meeker's face haunted Chipeta. The woman's cheeks were a ghostly color, and her eyes stared vacantly at her food. The pitiful woman was still in shock over her husband's violent death.

Chipeta gently patted Mrs. Meeker on the arm. She walked over to the wood-burning stove and lifted the kettle off of it. She carefully poured the hot water over the herbs she had placed into the silver-plated teapot. When the tea had steeped, Chipeta poured it into her fine china cups and handed one to Mrs. Meeker.

The woman nodded gratefully at Chipeta. Her hands shook uncontrollably as she held the cup and saucer in her hands. Chipeta stepped back to let her guests settle in. Her heart felt as though it would break into a million pieces. She tried to imagine the horrifying moments during the vicious attack, trembling as she did so.

When everyone had gone to bed, Chipeta lay wide-awake. Her body was gripped by fearful thoughts. She tried to imagine the things the Meeker captives had experienced at the hands of the White River people. The women and children were terrorized as the men forced them away from the safety of the agency.

She remembered Paron and his captors who had taken him nearly fifteen years before. There had been no negotiations for his release. Her boy was gone forever. Chipeta rolled over on her bed and tried to sleep, but the unwanted feelings of grief washed over her as she lay in the darkness.

In the morning, the Meeker group left the agency. Tears trickled down Chipeta's cheeks as she bid the women and children farewell. She wondered about their future and about the consequences the Utes would face as a result of the Milk Creek battle and of the Meeker incident.

Chipeta stumbled back into their house. She pushed the wooden door shut with her hand. The ominous feelings of an uncertain future consumed both her and Ouray. There was nothing the Utes could do but wait.

Once the Meeker women made it safely home, newspapers eagerly wrote of their harrowing experiences. However, the Meeker women remembered Chipeta's compassionate attempts to soothe their frayed nerves.

Josephine Meeker stated, "Chief Ouray and his noble wife did everything possible to make us comfortable. We found carpets on the floor, and curtains on the windows, lamps on the tables, and stoves in the rooms with fires burning. We were given the whole house, and after supper we went to bed without much fear, though mother was haunted by the terrors she had passed through. Next morning we breakfasted with Mrs. Ouray who shed tears over us as she bade us good-bye … "

On the other side, Governor Pitkin had spread panic by issuing a telegraph. It read: "Indians off their reservation, seeking to destroy your settlements by fire, are game to be hunted and destroyed like wild beasts …"

For days after the Meeker incident, the rumors continued. Some said that

Ouray had been unable to manage his people and that the Utes were killing and burning everything in their path. Newspapers printed banners saying, "The Utes must go."

Chapter 13

THE UTES MUST GO

CHIPETA CARRIED HER EMPTY bucket down toward the spring. Icy November winds blew dark gray clouds out of the north and across the wide-open pastures. Bone-chilling blasts of air cut through her shawl, causing Chipeta's teeth to chatter. She promptly set her bucket down and pulled the thick wool wrap tight around her shoulders.

The granite mountaintops of the San Juans in the south had disappeared under a thick shroud of clouds. The temperatures were dropping and the air smelled of moisture. Chipeta rushed down the narrow path toward the water. She stooped over the small seep and put her bucket into the frigid water. When it was full she carefully pulled it back out.

The Uncompahgre River, a few yards away, looked dark and murky under the heavy clouds. The ghostly silver-gray branches of the cottonwood trees creaked and groaned as the wind pushed and pulled at them. Chipeta hurried up the path toward the warmth of their adobe home. Soon it would be time to leave for the agency.

Chipeta's heart quickened as she thought about the hearings with Major General Hatch, Charles Adams, and First Lieutenant Gustavus Valois, who was a recorder and legal adviser. The men had been appointed by William Berry and the secretaries of the Interior and War to investigate the Meeker incident. Ouray, too, had been selected to the commission to help bring the men responsible for starting the attacks to justice.

Chipeta grew hesitant as she reached the house. The Meeker incident had plunged Ouray deep into despair. He had become even more listless and sullen. Thornburgh and his soldiers had ignored the repeated warnings to withdraw from Ute lands. Now the Utes themselves faced the negative consequences of protecting their rightful domain.

When she reached their house, Chipeta pushed the door open and stepped inside. A rush of warm air greeted her and she gladly welcomed it, as the temperatures were dropping outside. Chipeta set her bucket down and moved hastily toward the adobe fireplace. She picked up a piece of firewood and pushed it into the hearth with a poker. She stood back as blazing yellow and orange flames wrapped themselves around the log. Chipeta held her palms up toward the fire to warm them. She shivered violently as she thought of the Meeker captives and their impending testimonies.

It had been several weeks since their terrifying experiences, and she remembered their faces as they entered her home. Now, Mrs. Price; Arvilla and Josephine Meeker; Joseph Brady, the Los Piños miller; Henry Jim, a White River Ute who had acted as interpreter for Nathan Meeker; Captain Jack, the leader of the attack on Major Thornburgh and his men; Douglass; Johnson; and another Ute, Sowerwich; were at the Uncompahgre Agency to testify before the commission.

She and Ouray would attend the hearings, even though they were pessimistic about their outcome. In her heart, Chipeta was convinced that the men in Washington had already made their decision to move the Utes out of Colorado. The hearings were only a formality, she thought. They were the government's attempt to soothe their own guilty conscience about their role in the Meeker incident.

Her husband was in the bedroom dressing for the day. She had polished his boots and brushed off his suit coat. Chipeta wanted Ouray to look his best in front of the people attending the hearings. Chipeta laid her eyes upon the bedroom door as it slowly creaked open. Her eyes widened in disbelief as Ouray stepped into the parlor. He was not dressed in his traditional "white" clothes. Chipeta could hardly contain herself. Ouray was wearing the buckskin clothing she had made for him years before. Chipeta was taken aback by his bold move. Surely this would stir up bad feelings among the men and women at the hearings, but she kept her thoughts to herself.

As they made their way to the agency building, Chipeta studied Ouray as he moved slowly across the windswept grounds. His face was drawn and grimaced as he walked. All eyes were upon Ouray as he entered the hearing room. Ouray's dark eyes darted to the government officials at the table and then to the Ute men sitting on the floor. Ouray's face was stone cold, and he did not attempt to sit at the table with the other appointed officials. Instead, he sat down on the floor next to the Utes.

"I do not want to be a chief. I grow old and am tottering. Let some young man with the fire of his youth in his veins take my place. I have my farm, which I would rather cultivate and watch the seed planted by me grow up to maturity than to be head chief. They all come to me with their troubles. I know everything and have all their burdens to bear. Washington no want me to give up my position wants me to stay and govern Utes. I want only to be known as Ouray, the friend of the white man."

Chipeta stood attentively as her ailing husband addressed the council. It was November 16, 1879, and officials pressured the ailing leader to turn Douglass, Johnson, and Washington over to them for trial. She was flooded with relief when it was decided that Jack and Colorow would not be imprisoned for their part in the Thornburgh battle.

Ouray had refused to cooperate with the officials. He would not turn the others over to the soldiers. As Ouray continued to talk, Chipeta felt as though someone held their hands over her throat. Her neck was tight and she gulped for air. She could hardly believe that Ouray was severing his ties with the men in front of him.

Chipeta grabbed at her shawl as Ouray pointed his finger at Major General Hatch, Charles Adams, and First Lieutenant Gustavus Valois. "You three are all my enemies. You hate me … I have not one friend among you. You will not give me justice, and that is why I want to go to Washington where I will, at least, have one friend."

When the Meeker hearings were over at the Uncompahgre Agency, it was decided that the new Meeker trials would be held in Washington, D.C., just as Ouray had requested. Chipeta, Ouray, and the Ute delegates would leave for the capital city on December 29.

Chipeta disliked the thought of leaving their warm cozy home to travel eastward, especially during the wintertime. Ouray had asked her to accompany him as he traveled, and she had agreed. Chipeta did not want to be far from her husband. His health was too fragile, and she couldn't stand the thought of something happening to him while he was so far from home.

She trembled at the thought of crossing the treacherous mountains during the cold and stormy weather. Unwary travelers had often gotten frostbite or had frozen to death as they attempted to pass through the mountain valleys and passes during this time of year. Avalanches and deep snow were widespread, and the thought of riding to Saguache terrified her. Perhaps they would die on the way. Maybe their bodies would be buried under the deep layers of snowfall. Saguache was a few days from the Los Piños Agency II, and the trip seemed impractical to Chipeta.

The night before their departure to Washington, D.C., Chipeta and Ouray slept fitfully as they pondered the journey ahead of them. The recent Meeker incident and the battle at Milk Creek with Major Thornburgh weighed heavily on their minds.

Douglass, Jack, Sowerwich, and Johnson had still not been taken into custody. The White River camps were scattered throughout the mountains and valleys, and the deep snow hampered General Adams's efforts to bring the men in. Still, the general insisted that he would continue to pursue the men and bring them to Washington as soon as he could.

News of the raid had traveled from coast to coast, creating bad feelings within the non-native communities. People across the country hated them and any others who stood in the way of their progress. The panic-stricken citizens of Colorado had requested that the government remove the Utes from their state. Chipeta grew increasingly anxious as she lay awake in the dark.

The winds howled throughout the night, rattling the windows of their adobe home. Chipeta thought of the deep piles of snow outside their home and along the river. She feverishly wished that the army had agreed to wait until spring for the lengthy journey, but they did not. Major General Hatch had insisted that they leave tomorrow. Chipeta drifted into restless sleep, and she tossed and turned until morning.

When they awoke, it was five o'clock in the morning and pitch black outside. The wind had died down, but the weather was bitterly cold and

Chipeta's breath hung silently in the air. She shivered as she and Ouray dressed for their trip to Washington. Chipeta felt a sense of approaching doom as she stepped out of the house and into the frosty morning.

William Berry and Major General Hatch had already assembled the wagons. The buckboards were heavily loaded and their wheels had left deep grooves in the snow. Chipeta moved close to Ouray and grasped at his arm. Her heart beat furiously. Soldiers, too, had come to accompany them to Washington.

The soldiers had been ordered to protect the Ute people as they made their way across the country. They made the skin under Chipeta's clothes prickle. Images of blue-coated soldiers cutting down men, women, and children played out in her mind. She studied the soldiers again. The men chatted among themselves and cast a glance in the direction of the Ute riders. One man laughed as he spit at the ground. Chipeta looked away and down at her feet. She pulled her black shawl tightly around her distraught face and turned toward Ouray.

Chipeta shivered uncontrollably as the below freezing temperatures made the buckskin on her dress stiff. A deep chill seeped up through the ground and into her moccasins. Chipeta stomped the ground trying to shake off the cold and the horrifying thoughts of leaving her home.

She checked Ouray's robe and helped him pull it over his shoulders. Ouray winced in pain as he climbed onto his horse. His body ached constantly from his worsening condition, and he grimaced as he adjusted his weight on his horse. She mounted her pony, too, and wondered if her dear husband would survive the strenuous trip east.

Soon the rest of the Ute party joined in the procession. Uncompahgre Utes and White River Utes would be represented. Their faces were grim as they began to ride. The trip to Washington would determine their future.

Her body quivered at she thought of the people in Washington, D.C. Were they like the angry hoards of people in Colorado? Chipeta kept these last thoughts to herself as the horses and wagons continued to move at a snail's pace through the deep snow.

For six long days, the travelers made their way carefully through the valleys and hills along the Gunnison River. Wagons were repeatedly caught up in the deep snow, and the soldiers begrudgingly dug them out. Chipeta and Ouray said little as the party climbed into the hills and headed south over Cochetopa Pass. They pulled their robes over their heads and faces as blowing snow and ice pummeled against them. Horses too, were overwhelmed by the hostile weather. They bowed their heads low in an effort to stay warm.

The journey was extremely difficult since the weather conditions were unusually cold. Heavy snows blocked their paths over and over, but the group kept on going until they reached Saguache. Now they turned south toward the town of Alamosa, where a train waited to pull them eastward.

As they traveled southward, Chipeta breathed a sigh of relief. She welcomed the familiar terrain in front of her. It brought back pleasant memories, as she thought of her childhood days when her family had wintered in the San Juan region.

With the opening of the San Juans, thousands of people swarmed over the land like colonies of ants. They tore open the lands with their plows, ripping the growth out by its roots. They planted crops and put up fences, blocking pathways to the Utes' hunting grounds. Chipeta shook her head at the thought. She had been taught to honor the land and to care for it as if it were her own child.

Railroad workers broke the mountains into pieces with their picks and dynamite. Tons of rock fell from the hills, as echoes of blasting filled the hills and surrounding valleys. Thousands of workers rode the iron horses, laying mile after mile of the strange steel tracks—the very same ones they would ride upon when they reached Alamosa.

When the railroads came, the Utes had become apprehensive. The massive passenger cars brought too many people to the West. Men on the trains shot buffalo with their iron guns. They left their bodies to rot in the sun, while many Indian families on the reservations faced starvation.

After the railroads came the cattlemen driving vast herds of scrawny looking cows across the eastern plains. The creatures devoured the lush prairie grasses that the buffalo depended upon. Buffalo herds were left almost extinct.

Chipeta's dark eyes scanned the horizon. Clusters of small adobe homes lay nestled on the old homelands. She wondered about the people who lived there now. Where there had been wild and open spaces, there were now towns and communities filled with hordes of foreign people. Chipeta's stomach tightened as they reached the outskirts of town. It was January 7, and it had taken them ten days to reach Alamosa. Soon they would be boarding the train.

She gasped at the sight of the massive Denver and Rio Grand Railroad locomotive sitting on the steel tracks. Its enormous size took Chipeta by surprise. She felt tiny as she drew near the massive machine. Chipeta could even feel a rumble under her moccasins from the locomotive's engines. Her legs shook as she walked past the conductor, and followed Ouray, Otto Mears, Shavano (Ouray's brother-in-law and a sub-chief), Jack, Sowerwich, Ignacio (head of the Utes' Weeminuche band), Buckskin Charlie (the Southern Ute leader of the Capote band), and Severo as they climbed up the metal steps and into the passenger car.

Chipeta sat down on the bench and waited anxiously for the trip to begin. Inside and out, the train windows were encrusted in white ice due to the cold weather. She felt the car rattle as the engine began to roar to life.

Suddenly a loud, shrill sound came from the front of the train. The train's whistle startled Chipeta. She grabbed onto Ouray's arm as the train hissed and belched thick black smoke into the air. The car lurched forward and soon it was traveling past the station and out of Alamosa.

The car they were riding in wobbled from side to side as it chugged down the iron tracks. Chipeta did not like the jerking motion. It jolted her body back and forth. She was grateful for Ouray's gentle touch and smile as he tried to reassure her.

It was lunchtime when the train reached Pueblo, and the Utes and their escort stopped to eat at the train station. While they waited for their food, a fretful General Adams looked out of the window. Chipeta felt a knot in her stomach. She heard the muffled shouts of people outside. They sounded angry and threatening, and soldiers outside the station windows surrounded the building.

Chipeta looked at Ouray with frightened eyes. She watched nervously as

General Adams whispered quietly to Otto Mears and William Berry. The men's faces were suddenly serious. They grabbed their hats and quickly ushered the Ute party out of the station. Chipeta was terrified at the viciousness of the people.

The disorderly group reminded her of a swarm of hornets. She held Ouray's arm firmly as the citizens descended upon them, shouting insults and threatening to kill them. People threw rocks and lumps of coal at them.

Chipeta stumbled through the crowd, feeling panicky and disoriented. She lost her grip on Ouray as the soldiers pushed them forward to the train. The unmanageable mob closed in on the weary travelers, kicking and pulling at them. Chipeta screamed as someone struck Sowerwich down with a club.

Lieutenant Taylor and his troops moved into position between the mob and the frightened Ute travelers. Chipeta could scarcely comprehend the people's rage. She and Ouray had worked diligently to help these same kinds of people when they traveled through their region in wagons and on horses. They had hosted dinners and negotiated peace treaties, giving up the right to live in their homelands. Had their efforts been wasted? Chipeta felt a deep unhappiness in her heart.

Chipeta looked out of the window of the tiny compartment of the train as it continued to move eastward. The thick black coal smoke of the engine made the air hazy and dirty smelling. Chipeta felt unsettled as the train pulled her farther away from her familiar homelands. As they crossed the Great Plains, Chipeta thought of Paron and his first buffalo trip with Ouray.

Farms, small towns, and cities rushed past her at unimaginable speeds. She did not see the buffalo anywhere. Perhaps the rumors were true. She whispered to Ouray and he sadly shook his head. The men on the trains had killed them all. Chipeta leaned her head against the back of the bench and stared silently out the window. Her stomach protested against the constant motion of the train.

Chipeta tried to envision the people of Washington, D.C. Did they hate the Utes like Governor Evans and Colonel Chivington? Chipeta shut her eyes and tried to sleep as the train huffed and puffed across the landscape, carrying her hundreds of miles from her familiar and comfortable world.

Chapter 14

WASHINGTON D.C.

CHIPETA'S HEART RACED when the conductor announced their arrival at the Baltimore and Potomac Station in Washington, D.C. It was early Sunday morning, January 11, and the Utes had traveled almost 2,000 miles away from their home. The stress-filled journey had taken nearly two weeks. As the train came to a stop, Chipeta glanced at Ouray.

The thought of getting off of the train made her anxious. Chipeta was fearful that another angry crowd would be waiting for them as they disembarked from the train. To her relief, there were only a few passengers milling around at the station and members of the metropolitan police who had waited for their arrival.

As Chipeta stepped off of the train, her legs felt strange and walking seemed difficult. She felt as though she were still riding the great iron beast. Her body reeled from exhaustion, fear, and from her new environment.

As the agents and soldiers unloaded their baggage, Chipeta's dark eyes regarded the scenery before her. Ouray's detailed descriptions could not have prepared her for this moment. Everywhere Chipeta looked there were tall red and brown brick buildings with countless windows. Their tops disappeared into the low-lying clouds of fog and mist, reminding Chipeta of the cloud-covered mountaintops in the Uncompahgre Valley. She pulled her black shawl close to keep out the cold, damp air.

Chipeta climbed into an elongated carriage with Ouray and the nine other Utes who had joined them. When their baggage was loaded, the carriage began its jaunt through the city. As they made their way to the Tremont House Hotel, Chipeta could hardly believe her eyes. Even though the hour was early for the city dwellers, there were a few citizens who traveled in buggies and coaches, and by horseback. Wooden boardwalks ran alongside the roadways, where people walked side by side over the wooden slats.

Chipeta pointed at the curious-looking lampposts that lined the wide streets on both sides. Ouray explained that workers would come and light them at dusk. Chipeta listened in amazement as her husband told her how people of the city moved around at night. She marveled at the thought, and tried to imagine what the lamps would look like in the black of night.

When they arrived at the Tremont House, guests in the lobby paused and whispered to one another. They cast a brief glance at Chipeta's astonishing fringed buckskin dress, leggings, and moccasins. Chipeta's elaborately beaded scabbard hung from her belt, as well as another small bag. She wore beautiful silver bracelets on her arms, and a couple of rings. The people smiled at each other, and nodded toward Chipeta, making her face redden. She glanced at them uneasily and then followed the escorts to their hotel room.

The peace and quiet of their private room was welcome after the long and noisy train ride. The rest of the party had been assigned another suite down the hall. When she had put their things away, Chipeta encouraged Ouray to lie down on the bed. His face was haggard and his eyes seemed dim. Chipeta worried that the trip to Washington had pushed Ouray's body and mind to their limits.

She tried to rest herself, but her mind raced. Chipeta was apprehensive as she thought of Ouray's declining condition. She fretted constantly about the impending hearings and the impacts they would have on the Ute people. Chipeta thought about the hotel guests in the lobby and how they had stared at her. Tomorrow the streets would be full of strange people and the thought terrified her.

She regretted the fact that she and Ouray had come to the capital city at all. They were too far from the mountains and rivers of their homelands. There was nothing she could do to change the circumstances. Chipeta knew she needed to make the best of the situation for Ouray and for the sake of their people.

As Chipeta settled into life at the hotel, she calmed considerably. She had enjoyed meeting some of the representatives and their wives as they dropped by the hotel to visit with them. Chipeta was especially fond of Secretary of the Interior Carl Schurz and his lovely wife. They had invited Chipeta and Ouray to their home.

The furnishings inside the dwelling amazed Chipeta. In addition to fine draperies, chairs, and tables, there were other things that captured Chipeta's attention. She could not get over the chandelier hanging from the Schurz's ceiling. Its sparkling crystals cascaded down in brilliant glass rows. The crystal-clear prisms reminded Chipeta of the waterfalls that tumbled down the mountain slopes of their summer homelands south of the Uncompahgre Agency.

In addition to the wonderful décor of the Schurz home, Chipeta thoroughly enjoyed the kindness of Mrs. Schurz. She made her feel at ease in a time when the future looked bleak. Carl Schurz was so taken with the Ute couple that he recorded his feelings in his journal.

"Ouray and Chipeta often visited me at my home and always conducted themselves with perfect propriety. They observed the various belongings of the drawing room with keen but decorous interest and were especially attracted by a large crystal chandelier suspended from the ceiling. They wished to know where such a chandelier could be bought and what it would cost … Ouray was by far the brightest Indian I have ever met."

Everywhere they went Chipeta studied everything around her closely, trying to take it all in. The city was jam-packed with people, and Chipeta could hardly believe that some of them lived in the tall brick buildings. It puzzled her that they lived in rooms that were stacked one on top of another. As they continued their tour, men, women, and children gawked and pointed at the Ute party.

Chipeta could hardly believe the weird and wonderful dresses worn by the city women. Yards and yards of silk fabrics draped over the lower portion of their bodies and backsides, while their tiny waists were cinched snugly.

The eastern women lifted the front hems of their dresses in the air as they stepped into the streets or up into carriages. As they did so, they displayed layers of white, lacy undergarments and high-top boots that were fastened with a long row of buttons. The unusual clothing perplexed Chipeta. They looked awkward and uncomfortable to her. Chipeta looked down at her moccasined feet. She couldn't imagine wearing the tiny spiked shoes.

The women also did not wear their hair down around their shoulders like the Ute women. Instead, the ladies wore their hair coiled at the back of their heads in tight buns. The women, she thought, looked silly as they set large hats covered in fabric, fur, and bird feathers on top of their hairdos.

Shortly after their arrival, Carl Schurz decided to have the tailors of Washington fit Ouray and the rest of the Ute representatives with fine tailored suits. To Chipeta's dismay, he had even ordered a dressmaker to sew four dresses for her. In addition, Chipeta was given some of the strange-looking undergarments to be worn under her new dresses and a pair of the strange-looking shoes.

Secretary Schurz encouraged the Utes to wear their new clothing during their stay in Washington. The government had hoped that the new clothes would help the Utes fit in with the high-ranking socialites of the capital city. It would prove that the Utes were very much like them.

As Chipeta already suspected, the shoes and dresses could never match the comfort of her buckskin clothes and moccasins. The stiff leather shoes were too tight, and they were difficult to walk in. She hoped she wouldn't have to wear the uncomfortable clothes often.

In addition to the clothing, Chipeta was also offered tutors. She listened graciously while the tutors tried to educate her about the ladylike behaviors of eastern women. Even though she had learned a few English words, Chipeta could not understand everything the tutors said to her. She watched carefully as the woman demonstrated table manners and the proper etiquette expected of her when she visited the homes of President Grant and his wife, and the numerous other members of the upper crust. But even after her instruction, Chipeta still preferred her traditional Ute clothing and customs to that of the gentle ladies of Washington.

Some of the Washington aristocrats preferred her buckskin attire, too. They loved the wild, exotic look of the beaded buckskin dress and leggings Chipeta wore, and her odd-sounding language. Her stunning appearance thrilled her hosts and hostesses as she glided across their floors to meet them.

The people in Washington were fascinated by this woman, and they couldn't get enough of her.

All were anxious to meet the newest Washington celebrity. Newspapers and magazines across the country had fueled their imaginations by publishing rumors of Chipeta's heroic role in the Meeker incident. Writers recounted stories of a legendary 100-mile ride over "unmarked mountain territory" by Chipeta to rescue the helpless Meeker women and children. They stated that she herself had guarded the captives until help arrived.

Newspapers and magazines wrote constantly about Chipeta's first visit to the eastern city. Georgie Davis had managed a visit with Chipeta and the Ute people at the hotel shortly after their arrival. Chipeta found the reporter charming and was impressed by her artistic abilities. Chipeta stood near the washbasin as the woman sketched their images onto a white pad of paper. Her descriptions of Chipeta were flattering:

"Ouray and his wife glide in with noiseless moccasins while I am sketching and exchange some words with the rest, in a mixture of Ute and Spanish. The language and the voice of those Indians are singularly musical and the tones of the women have the softest plaintive sound, while her [Chipeta's] laugh has a quality of sweetness so rare among her white sisters.

She [Chipeta] is a stout and comely squaw, gorgeous in a red plaid gown and beaded leggings, her fingers loaded with rings, and wrists with bracelets, a fashionable white canvas bag hanging from one side of her belt, and a beaded pouch from the other, which last she slaps with a burst of merry childish laughter when Major Andrews points it out as her money purse.

The Major seemed thoroughly at home with his charges and thoroughly confident of the attachment and loyalty to himself. 'They are like so many children,' he says, 'I would trust myself twenty years among them.'"

There were some in the capital city, however, who disapproved of the Utes' presence. They expressed the same sentiment as the people in Colorado. A few of the newspapers touted headlines stating that the Utes were "unwelcome visitors."

With the written attention came the solicitations. Although Ouray was well respected in Washington, it was his wife's attention that the elite citizens clamored for. Invitations were sent to Chipeta, which she graciously accepted. The beautiful Ute woman had become a novelty among the upper-class citizens of Washington, D.C. They were wined and dined in the city while they waited for the hearings to begin.

Then, on January 15, almost two weeks after the Utes' arrival, the Meeker hearings finally began. For three months the United States representatives listened as the various witnesses were interviewed. Josephine Meeker, Captain Payne (one of Major Thornburgh's men), and Lieutenant Cherry told their side of the story, as did the Ute men on trial. The details of the hearings were similar to those heard at the inquiry at the Uncompahgre Agency in November.

Once the hearings had been concluded, the government made it clear that the Utes involved in the Meeker murders must appear before the commission. Douglass, Washington, and Sowerwich had not arrived in time for the hearing.

Finally, in mid-February, General Adams received word that the Utes responsible for the Meeker incident were on their way to Washington, D.C.

During the trip east, Douglass became disorderly, forcing the general and several other Ute men to hold him down. Douglass grew angrier and more combative, forcing the general to imprison him at Fort Leavenworth, Kansas.

Without their escort, General Adams and the other Utes continued the trip with Otto Mears and another agent, Mr. Lautre. News of the incident with Douglass disturbed Chipeta. It brought back the unwanted feelings of fear and panic. The Utes were still despised by people everywhere.

Once the White River Utes and their escorts reached Washington, hearings were resumed. Government representatives interviewed the men responsible for the Meeker incident. When the hearings were over, the commissioners decided that it would be best if the Ute people were moved to new reservations.

Chipeta felt as though she were in a horrible nightmare. She, Ouray, and all of the Ute people could not endure another move. They did not want to starve and die of the ghastly diseases on the reservation.

According to the treaty, the Tabeguache people would be allowed to stay in Colorado, but they would occupy the tiny area between where the Grand (Colorado) and Gunnison Rivers meet. Chipeta could not imagine leaving her beloved home along the Uncompahgre River. She loved everything about the valley. The thought of leaving it plunged her into despair. Chipeta hoped and prayed that Ouray would not sign the treaty.

To her dismay, however, on March 6, 1880, Ouray signed the first part of the treaty on behalf of the Tabeguache people, in hopes of staying in Colorado. If government officials found the land near Grand Junction to be unfavorable, the Utes would move to Utah. The Southern Utes would remain in the far reaches of southern Colorado.

The Ute people would own individual plots of land, as well as receive $50,000 a year to be distributed among all the people. White River Utes would not receive any income, unless they turned over parties responsible for the Meeker incident. Chipeta hated the fact that Ute lands would be sold to help compensate the Meeker victims and their families. She was confused by the government's resolution. Why didn't the government punish the few individuals who had caused Meeker's death? Why would they penalize all of the Ute people?

Ouray's signature was not enough to seal the agreement. In order for the treaty to become official, three-fourths of the Ute men needed to sign the bill. Washington officials and the Ute leaders agreed to meet again in August for another council.

Again, Chipeta tried hard to grasp the meaning of the treaties. She still did not comprehend how others could claim ownership of the land that Creator had given to her people so long ago. Washington suddenly seemed horrible to Chipeta. She no longer wanted to be there. She longed to be home in the Uncompahgre Valley, and she did not want to live anywhere else. There had been too many moves, and she was certain that Ouray would not survive this one.

Throughout their Washington visit, Ouray sought medical help for his condition. The doctor had informed Chipeta and Ouray that his state was terminal. The devastating news had not really surprised the couple. There were times during his trip that he could not even get out of bed. Ouray's body ached constantly and with each passing day he grew weaker and weaker.

On March 22, 1880, Chipeta, Ouray, and the rest of their companions returned to the Uncompahgre Agency in Colorado. The Ute people were distressed to hear that Ouray and the Ute leaders had signed another treaty. Now the southern leaders were expected to put their names on the documents, too.

Chipeta despised the fact that the United States representatives seemed unconcerned about Ouray's illness. They relentlessly pressured her husband to convince the Southern Ute men to sign their treaty. She hoped that they would refuse, and the Utes would keep their current appointed lands.

The Southern Utes had been cynical about participating in the negotiations. Without the help of Ouray, the arrangement between the United States and the Ute people was destined to fail.

The Tabeguache couple had talked a great deal about their trip to Washington, and about the politician's decisions. Still, Chipeta wondered if it was possible that Ouray had planned to put a stop to the treaty. Maybe he would tell Ignacio and his group not to sign the papers.

On August 14, 1880, Ouray, Chipeta, and her brother John McCook rode to the Southern Ute agency in Ignacio to speak with the leaders. Although he was weak and in a great deal of pain, Ouray had insisted that he visit the Ignacio Agency himself.

For three exhausting days, they traveled southward. Chipeta hovered over Ouray as they rode over the bumpy trails. She had pleaded with him, asking him not to go. She tried reminding Ouray that he was in no condition to travel; yet he had ignored her wishes. Chipeta's heart and mind revealed the truth. Ouray was dying, and he wanted to see his friends and family members one more time.

By the time they reached the agency, on August 17, Ouray's stomach was badly swollen and he had a raging fever. Chipeta promptly set up camp and helped Ouray lie down inside their teepee. She frantically tried to keep her husband comfortable while they all waited for the commissioners to arrive.

Upon his arrival, the interpreter Will Burns heard of Ouray's condition and went to visit him. The look of pain in Chipeta's face and eyes told him that Ouray's circumstance was serious. Doctors were summoned, and newspapers across the country focused their attention on Ouray's worsening condition. People talked about Ouray's state. Without their leader, the Southern Utes might not sign the treaty. Time was running out for Ouray and for his people. Chipeta grew more and more disturbed. Nothing she did could comfort her husband, or her for that matter.

Chapter 15

A TIME TO MOURN

CHIPETA STEPPED OUT OF THE darkened teepee and into the bright sunlight. She stretched her arms and legs and rubbed the back of her neck with her hand. It was still early in the day, and already the heat was suffocating. Tiny rivulets of perspiration ran down her face and back. It was August, the time when the crickets sing and the soaring temperatures make everyone sluggish.

Sleep had been hard to come by, as Chipeta dealt with the awful truth of Ouray's impending death. Her muscles ached from endless hours of tending to her husband. For a brief moment she was glad to be out among the living.

Nearly a thousand Utes from the seven different bands had settled in the area. Hundreds of teepees surrounded their own lodge. Chipeta understood the anxiety of the Ute people as they waited for news about Ouray, and of the arrival of the Washington representatives.

Chipeta brought her hand up over her eyes to shield them from the blazing sun. Even in the midst of death, she saw life. The sight of children laughing and playing along the banks of the Los Piños made Chipeta smile. It gave her momentary relief. The little ones seemed untouched by the momentous events taking place around them. Chipeta felt a pang of resentment as she thought of the children growing up on the far-off lands of another government reservation.

Women moved slowly through the encampment, trying to maintain their daily routines. Some carried water up from the creek in sealed willow baskets, while others tended to fry bread cooking in pans over the fire. A few babies slept soundly in their cradleboards, while their mothers worked with buckskin and beads.

Ute men gathered in large groups, smoking their pipes and discussing the impending treaty. They nodded to each other and waited patiently while each man spoke. Their faces looked tired to Chipeta. There was so much as stake. The lives of thousands of Ute hung in the balance, and only a small parcel of land remained under the control of the Utes.

The atmosphere of the entire village seemed somber to Chipeta, matching her own misery. She could feel the apprehension and unhappiness of the people as they waited. Soon they would choose a new leader for the Tabeguache people.

Chipeta closed her eyes for a moment. She imagined the wonderful times she and Ouray had when they lived in the Uncompahgre Valley. She could see his strong handsome face beaming when he had returned victorious from his hunting trips. She remembered sitting in her small adobe home as her husband hunted bighorn sheep along the rocky hillsides above their house.

A smile spread across Chipeta's tanned face as she replayed the years of their marriage. She fondly remembered Ouray's shyness when she first came to help Black Mare and Paron. Ouray had treated her well. He was gentle and kind, and soft-spoken. Ouray had respected her opinions on important issues—something she had always been grateful for. She cherished the long, cozy talks they had by the light of their campfire.

Even in the hardest times, it was Ouray who sought to comfort Chipeta. He had been quick to reassure her, telling her that everything would be okay. Ouray had promised to always take care of her. The last thought made Chipeta's throat ache, and she fought to catch her breath. Ouray would break his vow. He was dying now, and he would leave her soon. She stood in the village surrounded by people, yet Chipeta had never felt so alone.

The sights and sounds before her were of little comfort. Chipeta wanted to be tending to her everyday routines like the other women in the tribe, but she could not. Instead she faced a horrid and depressing scene inside her teepee, as Ouray lingered between life and death. She hurried back to her husband hoping she hadn't been gone too long.

When Chipeta returned, her eyes strained as they adjusted to the dark interior of their lodge. Buckskin Charlie quietly acknowledged her presence with a nod. He looked at Ouray, then back at Chipeta. He shook his head without a word. Buckskin Charlie's faced was grim and sorrowful.

In silence, Chipeta moved toward her husband. Even in the heat, Ouray shivered violently. His body was fevered and racked with pain. Chipeta whispered tenderly to Ouray and gently stroked his creased brow. He moaned softly at her touch and quieted. Chipeta remained close by his bedside as he drifted in and out of consciousness.

The flap at the doorway opened letting the bright light and heat into the teepee. Doctor E. F. Smith, the agency physician, quietly stepped through the opening. He had come to evaluate Ouray's condition. Chipeta frowned as the doctor lifted his strange looking instrument up to her husband's chest. Next he held Ouray's wrist, then laid it down. He left the teepee, and returned with two more agency physicians. Doctor Lacey (Ouray's personal physician), and Doctor Hopson (from Animas City, Colorado) entered the teepee. Their faces could not lie. It wouldn't be long.

A hard knot formed in Chipeta's stomach as the doctors worked over her husband. The two men hurriedly poked and prodded Ouray with their hands, speaking at one another in hushed tones. Chipeta winced each time Ouray cried out in pain. The doctors, she knew, would go to great lengths to keep Ouray alive—at least long enough to help with negotiations between the Southern Ute leaders and the government officials.

Chipeta's fading husband grew combative. He mumbled angrily and tried to lift his arm, yet his body had grown too weak. Ouray thrashed at the touch of the doctors. Chipeta tried to soothe him by speaking to him in a soft voice. The agency doctors stood back, in shock. Ouray had asked them to leave. He did not want any more medicine from the white doctors.

Chipeta scrambled to her feet. Her heart was filled with rage at the lack of respect for her dying husband. She looked down at him through tear-filled eyes. This was not the man she remembered.

Ouray, once powerful and lively, looked thin and aged. The agency doctors and their medicines had been useless. Even her homemade medicines had not helped him. Ouray was dying and leaving her behind, and nothing could change that.

The white men only worried about the treaty, and what would happen if it weren't signed. Chipeta had grown to hate the long and wordy documents— hundreds of tiny strange words filled page after page. The men in Washington had written them after councils with her people. Then one by one, the Ute men, including Ouray, put their marks on the lines making the treaty legal.

The treaties had done little to help the Ute people. They had caused nothing but heartache for her and Ouray. Whenever one treaty was broken, another one took its place. Ouray had been patient, and had tried to maintain a peaceful solution. Yet the trips to Washington, D. C., and the councils had been useless.

Ouray's faith in the government had been lost, and his spirit broken. Chipeta knew in her heart that this had hastened Ouray's condition. She motioned the agency doctors toward the door. She lifted the flap and requested that they go away at once, and leave Ouray in peace.

When the physicians had gone, Chipeta heard Ouray's feeble voice. It was barely a whisper. "Hear me both of you! Bury me where no white man will find my body." Ouray's words made Chipeta feel powerless. Her heart felt heavy, and it seemed as if the whole world was crashing down upon her teepee.

A few days before, Ute medicine men had gathered by Ouray's bedside in hopes of helping their leader. They had chanted and sang throughout the night, but their ancient remedies could not help Ouray.

For three days, the Tabeguache leader lingered painfully between life and death. Ouray's death was slow and agonizing. Chipeta could hardly bear to watch his suffering. Chipeta watched over Ouray, very seldom leaving his side. She wanted to spend every possible moment with him before he left her. It looked as though Ouray would die before first light. It was August 24, about mid-morning when Ouray made his wishes about the treaty clear. Buckskin Charlie listened to Ouray speak.

"I am not going to live long and I want you as head of your tribe to sign, that seems when you sign you'll get paid every year. After you sign first, the rest of the tribe can sign, next the chief of the Capotes, but the hardest one is the chief at Towaoc. I don't believe he'll sign.

We have good land here, plenty of water—don't let this land go. You stay here and take care of this land and work it. Buckskin Charlie, I don't want you to run around and leave your people. Stay until all your tribe dies and you die, too."

Wrought with grief, Chipeta lay close to Ouray's bedside and grasped his arm. She could not let him go, she thought. Yet death had a steadfast grip on Ouray, pulling him farther and farther away from her.

Tears welled up from deep inside of her. Chipeta could not, and would not stop them from flowing. She had been strong for her husband and for her people. Now she trembled with fear and sorrow. She cried for her handsome husband and his unrealized dreams. She grieved for the loss of Paron.

Sobs racked Chipeta's body. She grieved for the hundreds of Ute who had died at the Uintah Reservation, and for the children who went to bed at night with empty bellies. Her people had lost their ancient homelands. She grieved for the lost traditions of her people. The Utes had lost too much, she had lost too much. Chipeta's tears fell, her beloved Ouray took his last breath and slipped away from her.

An ear-splitting wail rose from Chipeta's teepee, making people in camp stop dead in their tracks. The eerie groans sent shivers down their spines as they realized that Ouray's life on the earth had finally ended. Everyone in the Ute camp quickly and quietly moved their lodges a mile away, out of harms way. They knew the ghosts of Ouray's relatives wandered near camp waiting to welcome him to the world of spirits.

Chipeta raised her voice to the world. She wanted people to know that she was in mourning once more. Nothing could compare to the pain she now felt. Ouray, the man she loved, was no longer among the living. Dazed and distressed, Chipeta removed her knife from its beaded sheath. She lifted the knife to her head and slashed at her long black hair. It fell into heaps on the dirt floor of the lodge.

As the cries continued, Ouray's widow slowly moved the razor sharp blade across her arms cutting into her flesh. Blood trickled down her arms and into her lap. The scars on her arms would always remind her of this dark day and the love she had for her husband.

The young Ute woman wept uncontrollably as she and her brother John and Buckskin Charlie prepared for the burial. Ouray's lifeless body was wrapped in saddle blankets and buffalo robes, and tied shut with ropes and cords. Next it was lifted onto one of Ouray's horses.

Death songs from Chipeta echoed throughout the day and late into the night. People in the encampment watched from a distance as Chipeta, John, and Buckskin Charlie rode away from the site with Ouray's shrouded body. They would take him to a secret place far from the white officials. They would honor Ouray's final wishes.

Ouray's body was laid to rest in a natural cave on a nearby mesa, along the Pine River. His saddle was shredded and placed beside him, along with a few of his personal belongings. Next a few of Ouray's prized horses were shot and killed, and left beside the grave, as well. They too, would accompany Ouray in the spirit world.

Several days after the burial, Chipeta gave some of Ouray's possessions away, including a few of the gold and silver coins given to him by the United States government. Shortly after Ouray's death, rumors had surfaced saying that Chipeta had thrown the gold and silver coins into the Pine River. They said it was a gesture of her disgust for the government's greed, and for their inability to keep their promises.

In keeping with the Ute burial traditions, the rest of Ouray's

An encampment in Ignacio, Colorado. Ouray and Chipeta visited Ignacio after returning from Washington, D.C. (Courtesy of the Denver Public Library, Western History Collection, #P-42)

belongings were destroyed, except for those possessions that remained at their farm at the Uncompahgre Agency.

In honor of their friendship, Chipeta sent Carl Schurz Ouray's finely beaded shirt, which he had worn during treaty negotiations. Chipeta explained that Secretary Schurz had done much to help her people. She considered the man a dear and trusted friend. Chipeta encouraged him to keep the shirt while he lived, and pass it on to his children. Ouray's beautiful shirt that she had lovingly made for him would signify their true friendship. He was moved by Chipeta's kind gesture.

As Chipeta continued to mourn in seclusion, Sapavanero was appointed head chief of the Uncompahgre people. Nobody knew what the future would be. The treaty had not been complete when Ouray had died.

Kaniache, the leader of the Muache band of Utes, often disagreed with Ouray's decisions, and he encouraged the other Ute leaders not to sign the treaty. Shortly after Ouray's death, Kaniache was struck by lightning while on the Southern Ute Reservation. Many of the Utes living there believed that his death was a bad omen, and that they should add their signatures to the treaty.

Still, the Uncompahgre Utes would not budge until Otto Mears promised to pay each Ute man $2 for their signature. The men agreed and applied their marks to the treaties. The Utes had given the government the last of their lands. They would soon move to another reservation set aside for them by the United States.

The final treaty indicated that the Tabeguache people would occupy the land where the Grand and Gunnison Rivers meet. The Southern Utes would remain in the southwest part of Colorado, and the White River Utes would be taken to the Uintah Reservation in Utah.

Chipeta, thirty-seven winters, was alone. She faced a lonely future without Ouray. She had asked to stay in their home along the Uncompahgre River, but Chipeta was told she could not own property. The government officials stated that the land and the house had belonged to Ouray. The home would be sold, and Chipeta would have to go to the new reservation with the Tabeguache Utes.

Otto Mears purchased part of Chipeta and Ouray's homestead at a very low price. He had given Chipeta a meager amount of money as part of her payment. Government officials were enraged by Mears's greed. They quickly insisted that he pay Chipeta $700 for Ouray's farm. In addition, they promised to build her a bigger and better home at the new reservation.

Ouray's widow was filled with despair as the couple's farm and livestock were auctioned off to the highest bidders. Strangers now owned many of their fine possessions. With only a few special belongings left, Chipeta prepared for the difficult journey ahead. Without Ouray, Chipeta's privileges and possessions had vanished like the buffalo.

BEFORE CHIPETA AND HER PEOPLE arrived at the new reservation, government officials had already employed "experts" to assess the new Ute lands. The men had decided that the location would not be suitable for farming and that the land was no good. In accordance with the treaty, the Utes would have to leave Colorado. The "unsuitable lands" became one of richest farming communities in the region. The government's deceit and gluttony had prevented the Ute people from keeping their legal lands in Colorado.

On August 25, 1881, a year after Ouray's death, Chipeta, her Mexican wards at the farm, and the rest of the Uncompahgre people began the long, forced march to the reservation in Utah. Soldiers from Fort Garland and Fort Crawford accompanied the Uncompahgre and White River Utes to their intended destinations.

Chipeta, along with 1,458 other Utes, moved slowly and steadily west past the old Uncompahgre Agency. There were no songs to be sung, and nobody rejoiced. There would be no more migrations to the summer camps in the high alpine meadows. The land before them was unknown, and its appalling history filled the Utes with terror.

People pressed forward as white soldiers holding rifles rode up and down the line on their horses, making certain that everyone was accounted for. The men barked orders at the people. They hurried them toward their unsettling future. Men and women were filled with grief and bitterness, while children tried to comprehend the reason for their journey.

Amidst the sadness, the autumn sun shone overhead. Trees in the valley had begun to change with the seasons. Their quaking leaves shone like gold in the sun. Chipeta paused briefly to take in the scenery. She wanted to remember the sights and smells of river willows and grasses.

She had always loved this time of year, when Creator painted the trees in splendid reds and yellows. She had spent hours in these meadows, tanning hides and gathering plants, while Ouray was traveling or hunting.

Tall and white against the sky, cottonwood trunks reached upward, standing like sentries over the *Noochew* as they silently moved past. Birds chirped and grasshoppers bounced back and forth across the trail. These were the familiar sights and sounds that Chipeta had known all of her life. She had grown to love everything about the Uncompahgre Valley and her Ute people.

Chipeta's memories haunted her as she moved on. She could feel the spirit of her people as they had lived and died in the valleys beyond her. Chipeta's thoughts turned to Paron and how he used to run along the Arkansas River, catching minnows with his pudgy brown fingers.

She reminisced about the time when she and Ouray sat side by side on buffalo robes twenty winters ago in the welcoming shade of the cottonwood grove as they contemplated their future.

Now, her moccasined feet moved silently over the old grass-covered trail along the Uncompahgre River. Chipeta's body and soul still reeled from the loss of Ouray and their home. Her feet moved methodically along with the others', yet her heart remained attached to the land.

Chipeta caught a glimpse of the chimney of their old adobe home. She shivered as a wisp of smoke rose like a ghost from it. Ouray had built the adobe fireplace with his own hands, and the couple stayed cozy and warm next to it during the

A Ute scouting party rides across the Los Piños River in southwestern Colorado, 1899. (Courtesy of the Denver Public Library, Western History Collection, #P-57)

long winter months. In her mind, Chipeta could picture Ouray riding in his prized carriage through the fields near their home. She could almost smell his pipe smoke when he greeted tribal leaders.

Now, all of their things belonged to someone else. A Dutch immigrant and his family lived on the farm. Everything the couple had worked for had disappeared like the smoke in the chimney. Chipeta felt a pang of sorrow and anger as she wordlessly said good-bye to the old homestead.

She was jolted back to reality as a soldier hollered commands for her to hurry. Chipeta stared straight ahead. She would settle among her people and return to the honorable Tabeguache way of life.

Chipeta decided she would not shed a tear. She would not satisfy the government's soldiers with her lamenting. She would walk proudly with her head held high. She would honor Ouray with her bravery. Chipeta felt the power of her thoughts as she continued moving forward.

When the Ute people reached the Grand River, they were loaded like cattle onto massive ferries and floated silently across the water toward an unfamiliar land. The people stood side by side, and children looked up at their parents with questioning eyes.

Chipeta loathed the scenery in front of her. Great, treeless plateaus of jagged sandstone rose up from the desert floor. Narrow canyons and ravines reached deep into the earth, making the hair on Chipeta's arms stand up. There appeared to be no wildlife for miles around, and water barely trickled in the creek beds.

Soldiers grew impatient as the people's pace slowed. The Utes shuffled over the rocky landscape, sidestepping cactus and yucca along the way. In the distance lay the Uintah Mountains, the northern border of their new home-lands and the hope for a more peaceful life.

Once they were past the reservation boundary, Chipeta sat down. She would go no farther. She would live along Bitter Creek. She did not want to be swallowed up by the Uintah Reservation. Chipeta wanted to be as close to Colorado as she could legally be. She watched as red clouds of dust rose up into the September skies, as thousands of her people continued to trek across the parched soil toward the dreadful reservations.

Chipeta could not have imagined this day in her life. She looked around at her surroundings. In her heart she carried a burden. Together, she and Ouray had tried to prove to non-natives that the Utes were intelligent and reasonable people. Her husband had spoken on behalf of their people and signed treaties hoping to avoid bloodshed and violence. Chipeta was filled with remorse and compassion for her people.

How would the people survive in these harsh circumstances? How could the government bring them to a place like this? Chipeta could not comprehend the government's reasoning. The lands of the Grand Valley would have served the people well, and yet the agents declared the land unsuitable.

Chipeta could barely see the Uintah Mountains in the distance. She closed her eyes and remembered Grandfather's story of the stick people ... long ago, *Sinawaf* had put the people in the Land of the Shining Mountains where they were to live forever. She was glad that Grandfather had gone on to the Spirit World. His heart would have been broken to see his people like this.

CHIPETA SAT ON A BLANKET IN front of her teepee at her summer camp near Dragon, Utah. She listened to the sounds of bleating sheep and goats as they wandered around the low, rolling hills along Bitter Creek. The morning sun felt warm upon her face as she whispered silent prayers to Creator. She asked that he bless the people with cooling rains, as the weather had been unbearably hot and dry. Chipeta's eyes followed a series of tiny dust devils as they swirled eastward across the parched alkali flats and brushland. She sighed in resignation as her mind conjured up marvelous images of the summer in Colorado.

It was late August, the time when everything was ripe—a time when she and the other Ute women would have been gathering cattails, wild spinach, and onions in the valleys and mountains of the Uncompahgres. Chipeta was sixty-five winters, yet her vivid memories of her life in Colorado made her feel ageless and alive for a brief instant.

Still, there were emotions of deep sadness and regrets as Chipeta thought of her last days with Ouray. It had been twenty-eight winters since his death, and Chipeta still grieved for her husband and for their beautiful home on the Uncompahgre River. She blinked back tears as she thought of Ouray's untimely death.

She had always imagined living in the Uncompahgre Valley and growing old with Ouray. She had hopes of watching Paron grow into manhood, too. Instead, she lived a life on the Uintah-Ouray Reservation without her husband or her son. Chipeta couldn't imagine Ouray or Paron living in the hostile environment that she looked out upon now.

She had settled along the western boundaries of the reservation, along with her adopted wards, her brother John and his wife, and Yagah, a longtime friend of the family.

She had accepted her 160-acre allotment from the government, and they built her sparse two-room wooden house that had not even been plastered or furnished properly. Chipeta had acquired a small table and a few boxes to sit upon. She shook her head silently. What could she expect? The government had not kept any of their promises since Ouray and the others had signed the treaty. The Utes had not even received payments for the lands they sold.

The year after Ouray's death had been particularly rough as she and the rest of the Tabeguache Utes tried to adjust to their new location. It had taken the people nearly two weeks to complete the long and exhaustive journey to Utah. It was September 1, 1881, when the solemn march began. The Ute people had been preparing for the move for months.

Women gathered plants and bulbs, and the men hunted deer, antelope, and other kinds of game to help sustain their families as they made their way to the new lands. The food had not lasted long, as there were nearly 1,500 mouths to feed and very few animals on the Utah lands. In her mind, Chipeta could still see the long line of dejected people as they walked along the dusty trail to Utah. The Utes arrived on September 13, and Chipeta remembered the long, cold nights they spent in the vast wastelands as they made their way west.

Life on the Uintah-Ouray Reservation was much harsher compared to their old way of life in the Uncompahgre Valley. The Utes were confined to the reservation and were not allowed to leave its

Chipeta holds Jimmy McCook (Roland McCook's grandfather). Jimmy's mother is on the right. (Courtesy of the Denver Public Library, Western History Collection, #X-30461)

boundaries to hunt for food. Men and women grew anxious, as the government's inadequate rations were often late. When they did arrive, the provisions were spoiled and full of insects.

The children's tummies grew round from starvation, and it broke Chipeta's heart. The government's promise to feed the Ute people had been broken over and over. Like the Utah band of Utes, illness and disease fed upon the deprived people.

Chipeta recalled her panic when she first surveyed the unfamiliar surroundings of their new home. She had learned at an early age how to identify and harvest hundreds of plants in her Colorado homelands. Chipeta's mother and grandmother had given her the wisdom when she was just nine winters, and over the years it continued to grow.

She knew the locations and the seasons in which the plants could be found. To her dismay, there was very little of the life-sustaining vegetation on the barren soils of the reservation, and there was hardly any water.

Outside elements were also an ongoing threat. Even in the confines of the reservation, Chipeta remained wary. The Ute people were still not safe from intruders. Trespassing missionaries constantly entered the reservation taking frightened children away from their mothers and fathers. The young ones were sent to boarding schools far away from home, where they were forced to live like non-natives.

Missionaries pushed their own ideals onto the Ute children, hoping that they would become more "civilized." The thought of it enraged Chipeta. She and Ouray too had tried to behave like the whites. The results had been disastrous. The willingness to adapt to non-Ute ways had been too costly for their people.

She wept as she thought of the young children lying in the strange beds at night crying for their mothers and fathers. The poor little ones were often physically and emotionally abused by "well-meaning" teachers. The truth of it was, the missionaries hoped to erase the Ute people's long and proud history.

Chipeta could hardly believe how the agreements had altered the course of her life and that of the Ute people. But Chipeta tried to take comfort in the fact that the Utes had been strong and resourceful. They had learned to survive and soon adapted to the new surroundings—just as *Sinawaf* said they would.

Chipeta picked up the tiny buckskin cradleboard and began adding beads to its canopy. She set her beads and her needles next to her on the blanket. The sun illuminated the tiny glass droplets, adding to their beauty. Chipeta loved the light-green, sky blue, and yellow colors of the beads. She enjoyed watching the geometrical designs take shape as she added row after row of beads onto the soft leather.

Chipeta held the cradleboard up to her eyes and examined it. She would give this to one of the little girls on the reservation, she thought. Chipeta fondly recalled the cradleboard her mother had given her when she was only two winters. It had been one of her favorite childhood possessions. Her mother had taught her how to bead during the long winter months. Chipeta's skills had improved as she grew older. It was a tradition that would never be taken away from her.

Chipeta added the final bead to her tiny cradleboard. She lovingly ran her finger over the delicate designs on the cover. Chipeta smiled warmly as she thought of the little Ute girl carrying her new cradleboard on her back. She would continue to keep the history of her people alive by doing good deeds for her fellow human beings.

CHIPETA REACHED FOR THE BLUE beads in front of her. She fumbled with the bowl, knocking the tiny beads all over her blanket. Her hands shook as she tried to gather them up. Foggy vision made it difficult for Chipeta to see. She had noticed the change in her vision several months ago, and agency doctors and medicine men had not been able to cure her condition. Chipeta hoped that the vision would clear up, but it didn't. Chipeta had no choice. She needed to see a new doctor in Grand Junction.

Hesitant at first, Chipeta had decided to visit Doctor Guy Cary. She grasped at the leather armrests on the chair in his office as the doctor examined her eyes.

Chipeta held her gaze on the physician as he spoke to her about her condition. She drew her breath in sharply as she heard the news. She had cataracts, and without surgery she would certainly become blind. The thought of being sightless petrified Chipeta. The sixty-seven-year-old woman couldn't imagine going through life without being able to see all of the beautiful things on Mother Earth. What would she do with her beadwork? Chipeta trembled as the doctor talked of surgery, but she agreed to the procedure.

Several weeks later, Chipeta returned to Bitter Creek, hopeful that the operation had made a difference. Shortly after her operation, Chipeta's eyes begin to give her more problems. Her eyes were painful and swollen. They were constantly teary, and her vision had not improved.

Desperate for relief, Chipeta traveled to Dragon, Utah, to visit Mrs. W. G. King, a nurse who worked for an eye specialist named Doctor Daniel W. White. They both worked for the United States Indian Service.

Chipeta spoke to Mrs. King through an interpreter. She sought Mrs. King's advice. The sympathetic nurse contacted the doctor in Grand Junction and received information on how to care for Chipeta's condition.

She gently applied hot packs and eye drops to Chipeta's sore eyes. Chipeta was grateful for Mrs. King's help, and she listened carefully as the interpreter explained the directions to her. In order for Chipeta's eyes to heal properly, it was necessary for her to continue the treatments.

Chipeta considered the nurse's suggestion. Her home was twenty-five miles from Mrs. King's home, and the trip was a difficult one. So Chipeta, along with some of her relatives, moved their camp from Bitter Creek to Dragon, where they settled along Vack Creek.

Over the next several weeks, Chipeta became Mrs. King's daily visitor. The woman patiently tended to Chipeta's eyes while Chipeta smiled sweetly at Mrs. King and patted the back of her hand. "Good friend," she said. The patient and nurse had grown fond of each other. When the eye treatments were completed, Chipeta gave Mrs. King one of her extraordinary beaded cradle-boards as a gesture of appreciation and a token of friendship.

As the years unfolded for Chipeta, the Utes continued to deal with broken treaties. Attempts had been made to remove the Southern Ute from Colorado. The government's efforts had been unsuccessful. People in Colorado and across the country had begun to change their attitudes about the Ute people. Many realized that the Utes, as well as other tribes, had been badly treated.

Chipeta's heart was gladdened by their new attitudes.

In 1911, lawsuits were brought against the United States government because of their failure to honor the treaty of 1880. The Utes had not received money owed to them from the sale of their lands, and many of

Chipeta, in her sixties, visits the old summer homelands near Ouray, Colorado. She sits on a horse next to her granddaughter, circa 1900–1901. (Courtesy of the Colorado Historical Society, #F-40200)

them struggled to survive in the harsh conditions of the reservation. Chipeta had voiced her opinion many times on behalf of the Ute people.

Newspapers printed the embarrassing details about the treaties and the impoverished people living on the reservations in Utah and southern Colorado. In addition, on August 14, 1911, the *Gazette Telegraph*, a Colorado Springs newspaper, published a story about Ouray's widow and the plight of the Ute people. The piece of writing found fault with the United States government for neglecting Ouray's noble widow for so many years.

As cries for justice for Chipeta were raised, her main concern was simply her eyesight. Her condition worsened. By the summer of 1913, her renowned beadwork was becoming more and more difficult to produce. When she worked inside her tent, the sixty-nine-year-old woman was unable to make out the colors of her beads. She depended upon others to guide her as she worked. Outside in the bright sunlight, however, Chipeta could see her beads and was able to work on her own.

As her sight declined, Chipeta visited Grand Junction again, in hopes of saving what sight she had left. The doctor in Grand Junction performed another surgery, and the results were disappointing. There was nothing the doctor could do to restore Chipeta's deteriorating vision.

However, even the government's policy to keep the Utes on the reservation and Chipeta's poor eyesight could not keep her from visiting friends who lived in Colorado. She visited her traditional homelands in Montrose; the town of Ouray, her husband's old hunting grounds; and Ignacio, where Ouray was buried. Chipeta constantly left the reservation for excursions to Colorado. She no longer worried about treaty rules.

In Montrose, Ouray's aged wife slowly walked along the Uncompahgre River near the couple's old farm. She reminisced about her days in the Uncompahgre Valley, and the wonderful years she spent there with Ouray.

The cottonwood trees on their old property had grown taller, and willows and lush grasses graced the banks of the river as it flowed through the countryside. Tears ran down Chipeta's face as she tried to focus on the landscape. The trips were bittersweet for Chipeta, as she missed Ouray greatly, and the lands that she visited were no longer Ute lands. Still Chipeta cherished the opportunity to visit Colorado.

In the last week of August 1911, the Southern Utes, the Tabeguache, and the White River Utes made a pilgrimage to Colorado Springs for the Shan Kive Festival. It was an annual visit that included sacred rites at the great Manitou Springs, and Chipeta too, had come to pay her respects to the Great Spirit that lived and breathed among the natural springs.

It was there that Chipeta was reunited with her dear friend from the Los Piños Agency, Mrs. Margaret Adams. Her husband, Charles Adams, the Los Piños agent, had died in a hotel fire in 1895. Together, the women remembered their past friendship and the time they first met. Chipeta loved sitting on Margaret's front porch and holding her hand. The two women had formed a strong bond between them.

Chipeta and Margaret rode side by side in a horseless carriage as the Utes paraded through Colorado Springs. Spectators lined up along Kiowa Street. They watched in amazement as the Ute leaders and their families, wearing magnificent regalia, marched proudly down the street. The crowds cheered as the celebration continued.

Even *Mah mah' que ats* appeared, flashing his fantastic black and white feathers. He called out to the Ute people as they continued to celebrate the gifts of Creator in the beautiful setting of the Garden of the Gods.

For days the people danced to the beat of the old drums, and their hearts were filled with gladness as their moccasined feet

Chipeta lived the remainder of her life on the Uintah-Ouray Reservation in a teepee. (Courtesy of the Denver Public Library, Western History Collection, #X-33928)

danced upon Mother Earth. When the ceremonies were done, the Utes left the hustle and bustle of the city and returned to their homes on the Uintah Reservation.

On her final visit to Colorado Springs, in 1913, Chipeta set up camp in the familiar meadows near the Garden of the Gods for the Shan Kive. She nodded in satisfaction as she sat in front of her teepee in the warmth of morning light. In gratitude, she lifted prayers eastward to Creator, thanking him for the time with her people and for their opportunity to come home again.

At night, as the younger people continued their dances, Chipeta lay still on her blankets in her lodge. She closed her eyes and inhaled. The mountain air was cool and sweet, and a gentle breeze whispered through the trees outside her lodge. The smell of piñon and sage, mixed with wood smoke from the campfires, brought a flood of happy memories.

In her heart and mind, Chipeta was young again. Her body was no longer old; she was a Tabeguache child running along the banks of the Arkansas River. Chipeta pulled the robes up over her frail body. She smiled at the wonderful memories of her early days in the San Juan Mountains. Surrounded by old friends and family, Chipeta drifted off to sleep to the sound of beating drums and chirping crickets.

Chipeta graciously poses in front of woven rugs and baskets, circa 1902. (Courtesy of the Colorado Historical Society, #F-1696)

Three years later, when Chipeta was seventy-three, she was

contacted by the offices of Cato Sells, the superintendent of Indian Affairs. He had heard of Chipeta's difficulties on the reservation. He felt badly that the government had neglected their promises to care for the Ute people.

Ouray had served the United States as a negotiator during the treaties. Chipeta had shown courtesy and kindness to white officials during their visits to their home at the Los Piños Agency, and yet Chipeta lived in the unforgiving environment of the Uintah-Ouray Reservation.

The government had forced Chipeta to leave her beautiful home on the Uncompahgre River. She had been promised a bigger and better home by officials, yet the reports of her actual living conditions embarrassed the superintendent. Chipeta now lived in scarcity on land where there was no water. The home the government had pledged to build was incomplete and poorly structured. Chipeta had abandoned it to live in a teepee.

Irrigation ditches were to be built by the government, according to their treaty, but the systems were never completed. The Ute people had tried making their own irrigation systems, as they had hoped to farm and grow fresh foods for their people. Sadly, settlers had built a canal upstream from the reservation. Water was used for their farms, and the Utes' source of water dried up, causing the farmlands to turn into desert. Chipeta and the rest of her family spent much of their time raising sheep in the mountains near Bitter Creek.

In 1916, Cato Sells queried about Ouray's widow, asking if she needed anything. Chipeta politely responded to the young man's question through an interpreter.

"I desire nothing; what is good enough for my people is good enough for me. And I expect to die very soon … and if I were to express what I have in my mind, someone would misunderstand and think that Chipeta's heart has changed and that she is no longer friendly toward the government."

Devoted followers sent gifts to the reservation for Chipeta. She received many things, including china and a trunk filled with luxurious silks. Chipeta had no use for those kinds of things on the reservation, and gave many of her gifts away, including some money that a well-intentioned person had given her. She could not understand the concept of the strange paper money. She gave the $50 and $100 bills to her friends and family.

Cato thought of Chipeta's situation. If she did not want fine china or money, what else could he give her? An agent at the reservation suggested that Cato buy Chipeta a shawl. The superintendent's gift arrived at Bitter Creek, along with a letter.

Chipeta, My friend,

I have read with great interest of the valuable services rendered to the whites by Chief Ouray and yourself at the time of the Indian troubles many years ago. I understand that your husband did everything in his power to stop the fighting and that you both made every arrangement for the comfort and welfare of the captives. It is good to know that these unfortunate conditions no longer exist but that the Indians now live side by side with the white man in peace and friendship.

To show that the government has not forgotten what you did at that time and as a slight token of its appreciation, I am sending you, through our good friend Superintendent Kneale, an Indian robe or shawl, with the request that he have it delivered to you with this letter. I hope you will like the shawl.

With best wishes,
Your friend,
Cato Sells, Commissioner

After the letter was read, Chipeta opened the package. She ran her hands over the soft folds of the fabric. The shawl, she recognized, was an attempt to apologize for the government's neglect. Chipeta willingly accepted the gift as a symbol of goodwill.

Thirty-five years after her eviction from Colorado, Chipeta took her own steps to open the doors of communication between the government and the Ute people. She knew that there must be a healing, and that the people must move on with their lives.

Chipeta sent Cato Sells a beautiful saddle blanket. She asked T. M. McKee, an agent at the reservation, to help her write the letter.

My friend,

Your beautiful shawl received, and was appreciated very much. In token of shawl received am sending you a saddle blanket also picture of myself.

I am in good health considering my age and hope to live much longer to show my friendship and appreciation to all the kind white people, and hope that this state of affairs exists though the rest of my lifetime.

Under separate cover you will find the saddle blanket, and hope that it is appreciated as much as the shawl was.

With best wishes I am always,
Your friend,
Chipeta

Chipeta's heart began to heal. She had accepted her life as it was, and tried to find joy in the everyday experiences with her family members. She had overcome many difficulties and had successfully survived the horrid eviction from Colorado.

By 1918, Chipeta looked for other ways to help the people on the Uintah-Ouray Reservation. She had shared her food, her home, and her wisdom with her people. Still, she wanted to do more. She remembered the $513 she had set aside in a bank account.

Even though she lived in poverty on the reservation, Chipeta insisted that the Red Cross accept her $500 donation. Representatives of the organization suggested that Chipeta keep the money. The money, she said, was unimportant to her and she gave the funds to them anyway. The donation was used to help the Ute people on the reservation during the great influenza epidemic.

By the age of eighty-one, Chipeta was totally blind. In addition, she suffered from chronic stomach ailments and arthritis. On August 16, 1924, forty-four years after Ouray's death, Chipeta too, slipped into the Spirit World.

Like Ouray, Chipeta was secretly buried in a sandy wash on the Uintah-Ouray Reservation, and most of her belongings were given away. People across the country mourned her passing. Newspapers wrote touching eulogies for Chipeta. No one could have guessed the impact she would have on the lives of so many individuals. Chipeta had lived a remarkable life with the Tabeguache Utes—a proud and noble people who had always lived in the Land of the Shining Mountains.

Chapter 19
CHIPETA RETURNS TO COLORADO

SHORTLY BEFORE CHIPETA'S death, a trader on the Southern Ute reservation, L. M. Wayt, suggested that a monument be erected in honor of Ouray. Buckskin Charlie and his nephew, Babe Watts, agreed. They would disclose the secret burial place of Ouray. Wayt petitioned the government to pay the expenses for the monument.

Ouray's remains were unearthed from their original resting place and brought to Ignacio for reburial shortly after Chipeta's death. Superintendent E. E. McKean of the Ignacio Agency suggested that Chipeta's body be returned to Colorado too, so that she could be reburied next to Ouray.

Chipeta's original grave was discovered shortly after her death by Albert Reagan. He spoke to Chipeta's brother, John McCook, suggesting that her remains be removed from the shallow grave and taken to another burial site. Reagan worried that coyotes digging at her grave would disturb her body, or that a rainstorm might wash the woman's remains away.

Citizens in Montrose heard of the discovery and requested that Chipeta's body be brought back to the couple's much-loved farm for reburial, instead of Ignacio. The town planned to build a large tomb for the renowned Ute woman.

Chipeta and the Ute people visited Garden of the Gods to celebrate the Moon Dance. (Courtesy of the Denver Public Library, Western History Collection, #P-1312)

John McCook gave his consent, and F. A. Gross, an Indian agent, helped make the arrangements. Chipeta's body was removed from its secret resting place near Bitter Creek and was put on a train in Dragon, Utah. Chipeta's body slowly made its way to Montrose, Colorado.

Unfortunately, the tomb was not complete, and Gross worried that Chipeta's friends and family would think badly of them. He wrote to C. E. Adams (editor of the Montrose newspaper) about the situation, urging the men to work diligently to get the site ready for their arrival. Adams wrote back:

F. A. Gross, Supt.
Fort Duchesne, Utah

Dear Sir:

Men at work on the tomb. Weather fierce, but we will have it ready. Wire when you start or when ready. We want to make the Indians feel we are in earnest and thereby inspire them to make a diligent search for enough of Ouray's remains to make a tomb for him (also). Better wire.

C. E. Adams
Montrose, Colorado

Even her poor eyesight could not keep Chipeta from visiting Mrs. Adams in Colorado. (Courtesy of the Colorado Historical Society, #F-40199)

On March 15, 1925, Chipeta's body finally arrived in Montrose. Her simple wooden casket was placed carefully on a horse-drawn wagon and taken to a local mortuary. Curious people lined up along the streets to catch a glimpse of Chipeta's coffin, while her brother John McCook, Yagah, Hugh Owens (agricultural agent of the Fort

Duchesne Indian Agency), and Reverend M. J. Hersey (a minister of the Episcopal Church where Chipeta had been received twenty-seven years earlier) followed from behind.

Chipeta's body was then taken to the site of the couple's old farm. Nearly 5,000 people, both Utes and the non-natives, had come to bid Chipeta farewell. The long line of people stretched out for more than a mile. In the quiet of the morning, John McCook, Reverend Heresy, and other important people spoke about their memories of Chipeta and of her faithfulness and courageousness.

Chipeta's body was placed in a large concrete tomb near a natural spring on the couple's old homestead. Chipeta was finally home, where she remains today. The natural spring near her grave had become an attraction to visitors. A concrete teepee was erected over the site shortly after Chipeta's reburial.

Another monument was built to honor Ouray, Chipeta's beloved husband of twenty-one years. The bronze oval portrait of Ouray was set into a stone obelisk, which stands near Chipeta's grave. These memorials still remain at what is now called Ouray Memorial Park, which is listed with the historical register. They honor Chipeta, Ouray, John McCook, and all the Ute people who once called Colorado home.

Although Montrose citizens tried to get Ouray's remains returned to the farm, their efforts were unsuccessful. On May 24, 1925, Southern Ute leaders reburied Ouray's body in the Ignacio cemetery, near his original homelands. After their deaths, Buckskin Charlie, Savero, and Ignacio were buried next to Ouray. In 1939, a massive monument was constructed to honor these famous Ute leaders.

John McCook died in 1937 and was buried next to his sister's tomb. A simple white cross marks the grave and says, "Chief John McCook." Sister and brother now rest under the blue Colorado skies, sheltered by towering trees as the sun's gentle rays shine across the old Ute lands.

Across the way, the Uncompahgre River continues to flow out of the mountains, as it has for centuries. *Mah mah' que ats* squawks from a nearby tree and announces the arrival of another beautiful day, and a new beginning for people everywhere.

AS THE FINAL PAGES OF THIS BOOK were written, I marveled at the fact that O. Roland McCook Sr., Chipeta's great-great-grandson, was in Washington, D.C., visiting the Smithsonian National Museum of Natural History. Roland had been recently appointed to serve as vice chairman of their branch of NAGPRA (Native American Graves Protection and Repatriation Act), helping museums and other government agencies find ways to return the remains of Native Americans and their sacred objects to their living relatives and/or tribes. While in Washington, D.C., Roland toured many of the places that Chipeta and Ouray visited 124 years ago. I found this to be a fitting tribute to his beautiful and intelligent ancestor Chipeta, and to the rest of his Ute ancestors who are now long gone.

Roland is a devoted friend of the Ute Indian Museum in Montrose, Colorado. Along with C. J. Brafford and the staff, he continually searches for ways to educate visitors about the Ute people and their enormous contribution to our national and state history. Today, visitors at the Ute Indian Museum can see for themselves Ouray's prized writing desk, as well as some of Chipeta's favorite possessions. There are tiny beaded moccasins and an intricately beaded cradleboard made by Chipeta herself. These fragile reminders of Chipeta's love for children and her people sit among other priceless artifacts. In addition, there are numerous historical documents and photographs of Chipeta, Ouray, John McCook, and countless other Utes who once lived in Colorado.

In August 2002, the mayor of Montrose made a proclamation honoring Ouray's beautiful wife. Chipeta Day was established and people from the three Ute Nations and from all over Colorado came to Ouray Memorial Park to honor her.

Everyone celebrated the day as an important milestone for the Ute people and for the Ute Indian Museum. It was an opportunity to heal old wounds. Smoke offerings from bundles of sweetgrass and sage rose through the branches of the old cottonwood trees. Drums were beaten, while Ute singers lifted their voices to their long-gone ancestors.

Many of Chipeta's relatives took part in the ceremony, including Roland. A long procession of tribal leaders reenacted Chipeta's funeral march, as the drums beat under the hot summer sun. Speakers shared stories of Chipeta's generosity and compassion. When the ceremony was completed, the Ute dancers, dressed in their finest regalia, demonstrated the old dances while the audience feasted on buffalo.

The little girl who grew up in the San Juan Mountains of Colorado so long ago has become a legend among her people. Her journey as a Tabeguache Ute continues through her stories, and her spirit is stronger than ever. A new quest awaits us all—one of truth and beauty, of understanding and of harmony among all people regardless of their ethnicity. Chipeta would have wanted it that way. Chipeta's legacy continues today through the lives of her friends and family, many of whom still live on the Southern Ute Reservation in Colorado and on the Uintah-Ouray Reservation at Fort Duchense, Utah. They have adapted to the harshest of conditions and made giant strides on behalf of their people.

An Osage Indian named Nompehwahthe once said, "Nothing can change what has happened, but history is what we make of what happened, and that means trying to see not just how we came to be where we are, but also where we are headed." Chipeta forgave the government and the people who had taken her people's lands from them. She always sought to understand her fellow human beings.

Ouray Memorial Park is part of the original homestead that once belonged to Chipeta and Ouray. (Courtesy of the Colorado Historical Society, #F-28,147)

The Council Tree

A poem Roland wrote speaks of the great Council Tree under which Chipeta was privileged enough to sit. The tree is seven feet in diameter, with its height reaching nearly eighty-five feet, and is believed to be 196 years old. It has stood throughout the test of times, as the Ute people's way of life changed.

Chipeta made history under that tree, as she was the only Ute woman to ever sit on the council. Chipeta and her ancestors are long gone, but like the Council Tree, their spirits remain. They live inside the young Ute children who are learning to speak the old languages. They live on in the men, women, and children who continue to dance to ancestral sounds of drums and songs celebrating their survival, long after *Sinawaf* first put the *Noochew* on the earth.

The Council Tree
by O. Roland McCook Sr.

*As a young tree I watched the Utes
come and go.
I have heard the laughter, the singing, the tired groans,
and the crying of the little ones.
I have witnessed the young ones as they played and
jumped from my young branches,
I have listened to the songs of the elders as the winters
move on and give way to spring and the happy
sounds of the spring Bear Dance.
I have sheltered the Utes as they hold Council beneath
my branches, the leaders speaking with wisdom and
foresight, the young warriors talking of war to protect
their hunting grounds and the Ute way of life.
I have stood here by the river for many winters since
the sounds of anguish and sobbing of the Utes as they*

passed under my branches for the last time, leaving the
Shining Mountains.
I have stood here listening and watching development
grow around my branches,
then,
I hear a familiar sound of long ago, and
strain my branches to hear more,
I hear the sounds of drums long forgotten
in this valley.
I hear the singing of the Flag Song, Round Dance,
Bear Dance, and songs that make
my leaves flutter in the wind,
I again see and hear the sounds of laughter
and the talking of Utes,
I am overjoyed to see the Utes are back, dancing,
singing, and visiting with relatives.
I stand proud as do the Elders who watch
from my branches,
I am the Council Tree.

NATIVE AMERICAN TITLES

Selu

Seeking the Corn-Mother's Wisdom
Marilou Awiakta
Foreword by Wilma P. Mankiller

ISBN 1-55591-206-0
15 B/W illustrations
6 x 9 • 352 pages
PB $16.95

"A book so wise and true it might have been written by Selu herself. And perhaps it was."
—Alice Walker, author of *The Color Purple*

Our Stories Remember

American Indian History, Culture, and Values through Storytelling
Joseph Bruchac

ISBN 1-55591-129-3
1 B/W map
5 1/2 x 7 1/2 • 192 pages
PB $16.95

Using both traditional stories and commentary, Bruchac provides insight into the totality of the Native American experience.

Keepers of the Earth

Native American Stories and Environmental Activities for Children
Michael J. Caduto and Joseph Bruchac

ISBN 1-55591-385-7
B/W photos, illustrations
8 1/8 x 10 7/8 • 240 pages
PB $19.95

" . . . a sensitive and well thought-out guide for helping children love and care for the earth."
—Joseph Cornell, author of *Sharing Nature with Children*

To order call 800-992-2908 or visit www.fulcrum-books.com • Also available at your local bookstore